The Great
CASTLES
of EUROPE

BARNES & NOBLE
NEW YORK

Contents

1 The coat of arms of Mary Stuart at Falkland Palace, one of the royal palaces of the Scottish Stuart dynasty.

2-3 Chaumont Castle, the feudal fortress of the Counts of Blois until the 15th century, was later rebuilt with round watchtowers and ornamented with conical roofs and Renaissance influences.

4-5 A marble staircase in the fairy tale castle of Neuschwanstein leads to the gilt apse of the Throne Room, which contains the painting Christ in His Glory and representations of six canonized kings and the Twelve Apostles.

7 The walls of Eilean Donan Castle housed one of the great Scottish heroes, Robert the Bruce. Pursued by the English, the future King of Scotland was given refuge by John MacKenzie, the Lord of Kintail. Once crowned king, as a sign of his gratitude, Robert the Bruce sent a lieutenant to the castle, transforming it into one of the most important royal garrisons.

Taken from:

CASTLES OF SCOTLAND -
Places and History
© 2001 White Star s.p.a.
ISBN 10: 88-8095-692-2
ISBN 13: 978-88-8095-692-1

CASTLES OF BAVARIA -
Places and History
© 1998 White Star s.p.a.
ISBN 10: 88-8095-467-9
ISBN 13: 978-88-8095-467-5

CASTLES OF THE LOIRE -
Places and History
© 1996 White Star s.p.a.
ISBN 10: 88-8095-878-X
ISBN 13: 978-88-8095-878-9

Preface

by Enrico Lavagno

One evening, at the end of the 15th century, a servant entered a room of Glamis Castle, in Scotland. It was Saturday and five minutes before midnight. The man begged the Lord of Glamis and his guest the Earl of Crawford, for the love of God, to interrupt the card game in progress: it was sacrilegious to play on Sunday. The Earl raised an eyebrow slightly and yelled that the game was not over and that, indeed, if the devil agreed he would continue playing with the devil himself until Judgment Day. The guests laughed, but it would be for the last time, because that game left them chained to the table forever, damned and invisible.

This is only a legend, but one that explains the fascination that castles hold for us. In that spirit, this book is dedicated to famous castles such as Glamis, which are perhaps the most characteristic creations in the history of post-Classical West, offering a guide in images and words of the most notable examples to be found in Europe in this field.

The problem is the variety, so rich and diverse because Europe, as the soul of the Old World, is the place where castles took their shape and name between the 5th and 6th centuries, in the fading light of the sunset of both the Ancient World and the Roman Empire. For this reason the pages that follow limit themselves to the most important centers, to historical regions that were, and in certain respects still are, transmitters of unmistakable messages of dominion and supremacy that the castles spread to neighboring lands.

Scotland, the Loire Valley, Bavaria: in these places, in different times and ways, the most important chapters in the history of the West were written, this same history that spurred the emergence of some of the most famous castles in the world, finding their natural and perfect counterparts there. And just as much, the resplendent walls of Chenonceaux, Amboise and Neuschwanstein, no less than the gloomy ones of Glamis and Holyrood, are not only part of great history and events of continental significance, but are also part of the chronicle of daily life, with the biography of the characters and with the psychology of the individuals. Within the walls of the castle are found not only memories of wars that were planned there, peace treaties signed there, sieges suffered, but also the lives of lords and ladies, of troubadours, of alchemists and artists, of servants, of garrisons in the guardrooms and of farmers who supplied the castles and who took refuge in them in times of danger.

The stones of *castrum* architecture have the characteristic of reflecting different visions of the world, besides different personal and collective lives. Indeed, there is no one model of a castle, but many, each one adapted to its own natural and human panorama. That is why this "walk through the castles" offers flashes of immediate understanding of complex and even dull matters: each nation that built castles has transposed its own character on them. Take Bavaria, for example. The singular absence of any Renaissance characteristics in Bavarian castles has a precise explanation.

9 Neuschwanstein Castle was never completed: the entire second floor, which is not open to the public, consists of empty rooms and bare brick walls.

8

10-11 Cheverny Castle, made of Bourré stone with slate roofs, is an architectural ensemble with a classical style that marks a development in the evolution of the Loire châteaux.

10 top The large drawing room, in Louis XIII style, contains a wealth of furnishings, from the large red carpet at the foot of the fireplace to the furniture and decorations in blue and pure gold.

12-13 At the center of the southern façade of the entrance portico is set the white marble coat of arms of Prince Albert, while at the foot of the western side is the foundation stone laid by Queen Victoria on the 28th of September, 1853.

14-15 The Bed Chamber in the Rich Rooms of the Munich Residenz was used as a direct model for the Bed Chamber at Linderhof, which is shown in the picture. Despite their similarities, in particular the bed alcove with its magnificent gold embroidery, there are significant differences, especially in the frescoed ceiling of Linderhof, which does not appear in Cuvilliés' original model.

In terms of economics and human life, the Thirty Years' War cost the nation so dearly that it wiped out the workforce and the circulation of funds necessary to build and develop the kingdom. Conversely, in France, the kings were able to afford and promote national development. In Bavaria, next to large Baroque castles we find Romanesque and Gothic castles among the biggest on the Continent, places in which the knights of long ago still felt at home, reflecting elements of the population and economy entirely devoted to the destructive and often devastating military arts of the Middle Ages.

Scotland, for its part, contributed more than the rest of Europe to creating the special mythology of castles, having some that have maintained their original appearance of sentinels at the edge of the world, rising stone upon stone, stark and forbidding. The idea of Scotland seems inseparable from that of the castle, which in that land has ancient roots, dating back to the Late Neolithic period and the Bronze Age. And yet, even in a land that in many areas is lightly populated and often of poor soil, abundance is seen in the mixture of ideas from very different populations, from the peaceful pre-Celts to the ingenious Celts, from the Roman invaders to the terrible Saxons and Vikings, up to the Normans, who one after other transferred to this land their own conceptions of defense and of human and courtly affairs. One result was the building of brochs, isolated cylindrical towers dating from before the time of Christ; another is the compact buildings that belonged to the hereditary aristocracy of the medieval Highlands, whose primary defensive function is leavened with the beauty of legend and landscape. Many of these earlier structures are not far from lavish Victorian castles, which are more often oversized country residences than defensive facilities.

In contrast to the Bavarian and Scottish situations, the Loire Valley reflects the economic miracle of post-Roman France, which made the country the most stable European power up to modern times. Hence the dark Medieval fortresses that were quickly transformed into the famous castles of the kings of France. They were fabled even in their own time, luminous jewels of refinement in which the absolute monarchs amused themselves by keeping the illustrious minds of their times in gilded prisons amid the sites of sumptuous courts and memorable feasts.

Turning pages of stone to read history has the advantage of immersing the visitor in an odd place in time that is neither legend nor history, but both, and that lives in the creaking of ceiling beams, in the wind on the walls, in the atmosphere of secrets. From one stone to another, from one page to the next, this book lowers drawbridges across time, telling stories of departed men and of events long past. Without this ephemeral transit between fortress and castle we would lose a part of ourselves and forgo the delights of imagination rekindled.

Castles of Scotland

SECTION ONE

16-17 Drummond Castle, with its famous garden, is located in Central Scotland. It stands on a rise and the terraces overlook the marvellous and painstakingly groomed lawns laid in the form of the cross of St Andrew. The sundial in the center dates from 1630.

18 top Eilean Donan Castle, one of the most spectacular in Northern Scotland, takes its name from the island on which it stands. Part of the castle was built in 1220 by Alexander II as a defensive fortress against the Vikings. Later, Alexander III presented it to Colin Fitzgerald, the son of the Irish Earl of Desmond, the ancestor of the McKenzies.

19 top Castle Stalker on the West Coast between Oban and Fort William is an austere tower house built in the middle of the 16th century and the home of the Stewarts of Appin. Surrounded by wild landscapes of immense appeal, the castle protected the banks of Loch Linnhe from the attacks of enemy clans.

19 bottom Set on the small island of Mousa off South Mainland, the largest of the Shetland Islands, Mousa Broch is perhaps the best preserved of the over two hundred defensive structures dating from the beginning of the Iron Age present in Scotland. When the brochs were no longer needed for defence they were used as the basis for settlements and the agricultural exploitation of the land.

From the establishment of the kingdom of the Scots under King Kenneth MacAlpine in 843 to the Union with the English Crown in 1707, all of the Scottish castles played a principally defensive role. High, turretted and surrounded by walls and bastions they were apparently impregnable and as well as protecting the local lord, served as his administrative center and the residence of his family, servants and soldiers. The fortified tower, or tower house, was the most common form and was found in both the remote Highlands and the fertile valleys of the Borders, at the confine with England. Composed of three storys linked by spiral staircases in stone or wood, the last of which was overhanging, the tower house was a feature of over 1000 years of Scottish history, from the defensive towers of the Picts and the Scots to the noble palaces of the Victorian era. The form evolved over the centuries with the addition of new elements, but the most fascinating examples are those that have managed to retain the characteristic tower motif. Many have survived such as Threave Castle in Dumfries and Galloway, one of the oldest, and the castles of Craigmillar and Crichton, which were originally two tower houses successively extended. The earliest Scottish fortifications date back to the Iron Age. Between 800 BC and 400 AD there were numerous hill forts, earthworks or stone walls constructed to defend the villages from the neighboring tribes or the incursions of the Romans (AD 71-84). One of the most famous hill forts is located at Dunnadd in Argyll, the ancient capital of the kingdom of Dalriada. Another form of defensive structure were the brochs, tall towers with double walls in stone, cylindrical in form and tapering slightly towards the top. In spite of the Scandinavian origin of their name, the brochs were built long before the arrival of the Norwegians and probably co-existed with the hill forts. They were over thirty-three feet high and were inhabited by the ruling family, but in times of danger they could accommodate up to two hundred persons. Among the best conserved brochs is that of Mousa in the Shetland Islands.

21 top left The isolated ruins of Crichton Castle stand on the bank of the River Tyne, at the foot of Moorfoot Hills in the Lothian region close to Edinburgh. Built in the 14th century and extended during the following two centuries, the castle was the home of Sir William Crichton, the Scottish Chancellor during the reign of James II.

21 bottom right The magnificent gardens of Edzell Castle were created in 1604 by Sir David Lindsay. The Pleasance is a formal garden surrounded by walls in sculpted stone, pots of flowers and niches for birds. The ruined tower house dates from the 15th century. In 1562 Mary Stuart held a council here during the royal army's campaign against the Gordons.

20 top left Caerlaverock Castle has an unusual triangular plan and it conceals an internal façade with symmetrical Renaissance decoration. The principal elements are the semi-circular or triangular windows and the pediment of the doorway sculpted with mythological or heraldic motifs.

20 top right In the 13th century at St. Andrews, on the North coast of the Fife peninsula, a fortified bishop's palace was constructed in which James I and James III were educated. St. Andrews Castle was at the center of the conflict during the religious wars and was almost completely demolished to provide material for the construction of the port's sea-wall.

20-21 and 21 top right The aerial view shows Crathes Castle and its beautiful gardens. Yew hedges separate the Color Garden in which the dominant colors are yellow, red and violet, from the more formal Fountain Garden, based on blue, and the Rose Garden. The most recent creation is the Golden Garden dedicated to the memory of Lady Burnett who was responsible, together with her husband Sir James, for this green oasis.

In 1066 the marriage between Malcom III Canmore and Margaret, who was raised at court in London, brought Norman customs and traditions to the wild Scotland. The first feudal castles date from this period. The earliest examples took the form of mounds dominated by a wooden tower and surrounded by a moat, at the foot of which stood wooden houses within a courtyard surrounded by a palisade. There are no surviving examples of this "motte-and-bailey" castle, but they are clearly depicted in the Bayeux Tapestry. At Hawick in the Borders, however, the earth mound on which the wooden tower once stood can still be seen. Over the course of the following two centuries stone castles almost completely replaced the old wooden structures. In a number of the castles constructed after the mid-fourteenth century there was an evident desire to improve the defensive capabilities that previously relied exclusively on the buildings' massive structure. In the castle of St. Andrews in Fife, for example, the tower is no longer set in the middle of the bailey and the principal entrance to the castle is incorporated within it. At the end of the fifteenth century decorative and ornamental elements began to increase in importance, especially in the royal residences. The richness of these constructions drew heavily on French Renaissance motifs, probably due to the alliances and close ties of kinship between the Stuarts and the French royal family in that period.

Falkland Palace, James V's favorite residence, has nothing in common with the original tower house, embellished as it is with a wealth of towers, turrets, medallions and pilasters. The sculptural decoration of the North Wall of Crichton Castle in the Borders region, completed in 1585, was moving in the same direction, as was Caerlaverock Castle in Dumfries, in which the massive, austere exterior contrasts with the elegance of the internal courtyard.

22 top left Aerial view of Culzean Castle on the West Coast, a few miles from the city of Ayr. Standing on the cliff-top, this is one of the most impressive stately homes in the whole of Scotland, the fruit of the creative genius of Robert Adam who designed it in the 18th century to replace the existing 200-year-old castle.

22 top right Austere and turreted, the Gothic Revival Abbotsford House, the home built by Sir Walter Scott, stands on the River Tweed, a short distance from Melrose. The writer responsible for the

invention of Romantic Scotland and the author of novels set in the Highlands such as Rob Roy, Ivanhoe and The Pirate was so attached to these lands that he built his ideal house here.

22-23 An aerial view of Balloch Castle, the ancient home of the Lennox family. Set in a great park on the shores of Loch Lomond in Western Scotland, the castle was built in 1808 in the Gothic Revival style. Fine

views of the lake and the gardens with the attractive contrast between the Mediterranean plantings and the wild nature of the mountains can be enjoyed from the house.

23 top The library in Mellerstain House is one of Robert Adam's masterpieces. The main feature is the stuccoed ceiling that still retains the delicate pastel colors of pale green, dark green and pink specified by the architect in 1773. A round painting of Minerva by Zucchi decorates the circular medallion. Robert Adam was also responsible for the white and green fireplace and the mirror cupboards between the windows.

23 bottom The sitting room of Dalmeny House, the Gothic Revival house overlooking the Firth of Forth on the outskirts of Edinburgh, is furnished with French furniture that was once part of the collection of the Rothschilds of Mentmore and came to Dalmeny through the marriage of the 5th Earl Archibald, Prime Minister between 1894 and 1895, and Hannah, the daughter of Baron Meyer de Rothschild of Mentmore.

This greater attention to the external appearance of the buildings led to the development of the ornamental potential of the defensive elements. This tendency can be seen in the castles built in the Northeast of Scotland from the late sixteenth century. Castles such as those of Crathes and Fyvie are at the same time both fortresses and elaborate works of art. With the Act of Union of 1707 the Scottish castles' defensive function was made largely redundant. Although for 40 years, up to the massacre of Culloden, the Jacobites maintained their opposition to the Crown, Scotland enjoyed a period of peace. The families of the old nobility, made even richer by the expropriation of terrain from the small landowners, began to build great palaces. They were then flanked by the families of the great merchants and those of the early industrialists who commissioned leading architects to build their homes. The years between the eighteenth and the nineteenth centuries saw the establishment of a successful architectural dynasty, the Adams, sensitive to neo-classical and Italian influences. Among the Adam family's most important creations were the beautiful Charlotte Square in Edinburgh, Hopetoun, Mellerstain and Culzean Castle, characterized by extremely simple, clean external lines contrasting with the opulence of the interiors. In the second half of the last century, thanks to the novels of Sir Walter Scott, Romanticism led to a revival of interest in the Medieval world and the

Scottish traditions. Architecture was not immune to this new trend and the period saw the construction of houses decorated with towers, ogives and dark inlaid wood. Sir Walter Scott's own residence, Abbotsford, and Dalmeny House are good examples, while Balmoral Castle, the royal family's summer residence, remains the best example of the neo-baronial style, the leading exponents of which were the architects David Bryce and Gillespie Graham.

Mellerstain House

Scone Palace

Drum Castle

26-27
Castle Tioram,
the powerful castle
belonging to the
MacDonalds of
Clanranald was
built early in the
14th century on a
remote island in
Loch Moidart.
Accessible by land
only at low tide, it
was frequently
attacked by the rival
Campbell clan and
was burned down
in 1715.

28-29 The impressive
library of Dunrobin
Castle built by Sir
Robert Lorimer,
contains over ten
thousand volumes,
with numerous rare
and precious editions.
Most of the works are
concerned with the
development of the
Highlands and
Scottish law.
There is also a fine
Chippendale desk and
a 19th-century globe.
A portrait of the
Duchess Eileen Butler
who married the
Duke of Sutherland
in 1912 hangs on the
wall. There is a
precious oriental
carpet on the floor.

Thirlestane Castle

Caerlaverock Castle

Castle Fraser

Atlantic
Ocean

Orkney
Islands

North
Sea

Outer Hebrides

Thurso

Dunrobin Castle

Oykel

The Highlands

Dunvegan
Castle

Brodie Castle

Cawdor Castle

Fyvie Castle

Haddo House

Inverness

Spey

Deveron

Isle
of Skye

Don

Castle
Fraser

Drum Castle

Loch Ness

Craigievar Castle

Aberdeen

Caledonian Canal

Grampian Mountains

Balmoral

Crathes Castle

Fort
William

Braemar

Dunnottar Castle

Loch
Linnhe

Blair Castle

Glamis Castle

Castle
Stalker

Tay

Dundee

Mull

Scone Palace

Perth

Oban

St. Andrews

Inveraray Castle

Drummond Castle

Falkland Palace

Loch Lomond

Hopetoun
House

Stirling Castle

Edinburgh

Atlantic
Ocean

Linlithgow
Palace

Edinburgh Castle
Holyrood

Glasgow

Thirlestane Castle

Mellerstain House

Brodick
Castle

Tweed

Traquair House

Floors Castle

Ayr

Abbotsford House

Teviot

Arran

Culzean Castle

Drumlanrig Castle

Esk

Northern
Ireland

North Channel

Dee

Dumfries

Caerlaverock
Castle

England

THE CASTLES OF
MARY QUEEN OF SCOTS

*30 top A portrait of
Mary Stuart, Queen of
Scotland and pretender
to the throne of
Elizabeth I. The sword,
the scepter and the jewels
worn by the Queen are
today conserved in
Edinburgh Castle.*

*30 bottom Mary Stuart
became Queen just after
her birth, because of the
death of her father,
James V. Before Mary
was three years old, the
English king Henry VIII
sent an army to demand
the fulfilment of the
marriage proposal
between his son Edward
and Mary. The episode
is known in history as
the "rough wooing."*

*30-31 Linlithgow
Palace dominates the
town and the small lake.
Although it is now
roofless, this impressive
building is still in a fair
state of preservation.
Of great beauty, its
central courtyard is
a concentration of
centuries of Scottish
history with the
extensions and additions
built at the behest of
diverse monarchs of the
Stuart dynasty. The
Stuarts were
accustomed to spending
long periods in this
palace.*

Mary Queen of Scots, the heir to the powerful Stuart dynasty that had long fought against England and had brought sophisticated architecture and tastes to the Scottish court, came to the throne during the tragic years of the religious struggles between Catholics and Protestants. The daughter of James V and the French Princess, Mary of Guise, Mary Stuart had a turbulent life of love and betrayal, intrigue and assassinations that have made her a legendary figure. She was born on the 8th of December, 1542, at Linlithgow Palace, one of the Stuarts' favorite residences on the shores of the Firth of Forth, mid-way between Edinburgh and Stirling. With its powerful red towers reflecting in the water, the castle was built in 1425 by James I on his return to Scotland after eighteen years of imprisonment in England. His successors introduced modifications and refurbishments that transformed the castle into a palace rivalling those of France, as was confirmed by Queen Mary of Guise. The diverse styles of the façades facing the interior courtyard recount the history of the palace: to the east is the Great Hall and the original entrance of James I, to the north the new wing built by James IV, to the west the state apartments added by James III and to the south the English-style façade built by the sovereign and the queen Margaret Tudor.

Mary's father, James V, died of a heart attack just six days after her birth.

32 center left and right At the center of the struggle for independence, Stirling Castle was retaken by the Scots in 1297 thanks to William Wallace (photo on the right) following the Battle of Stirling Bridge, then a wooden structure linking the north and south of Scotland. Having been regained by the English and retained for ten years, in 1324 it was again conquered by Robert the Bruce at the Battle of Bannockburn.

32 bottom left Stirling Castle was built in its present form between the end of the 14th and the 16th centuries. James IV ordered the building of the Great Hall and the gatehouse. James V on the other hand was responsible for the spectacular palace, built with the help of French masons. James VI, at whose behest the Royal Chapel was built, was the last Scottish sovereign to reside in the castle.

32 top left and 33 Following the moat and the first gateway to Stirling Castle, the road climbs to the internal gateway. A ramp on the left leads to the Queen Anne Gardens while a third entrance opens onto Lower Square overlooked by the royal palace with its decorated façade, a masterpiece in the Renaissance style. Together with the palaces of Falkland and Linlithgow, this is one of the few examples of how the ideas of the European Renaissance found expression in Scotland.

The coronation of the infant Mary took place in the austere castle at Stirling where she lived until she departed for France as the fiancée of the Dauphin at just five years of age.

Set in a strategic position on the principal road linking the north and south of Scotland, Stirling was already fortified in prehistoric times. Through here passed all the Scottish kings, including Alexander I and William the Lion who also died here. Significant battles in Scottish history were fought around the castle, including that of Stirling Bridge in 1297 when the Scots, led by William Wallace, defeated the English army. Attacked on a number of occasions by the English during the wars of independence, Stirling was the last Scottish fortress to surrender in 1304. With the Stuart dynasty the castle became a royal palace, as can still be seen today. James II reinforced the defences, lending the castle its severe, invincible air, but he also constructed the Great Hall to house the Scottish Parliament and State ceremonies. James IV began work on the Renaissance-style royal palace eventually completed by his son James V who was crowned in the chapel of Stirling Castle, as was later the case with his daughter Mary and his grandson James VI in 1566.

Mary spent her childhood and youth in France in order to escape the wars with England. Educated in the luxury of the French court, in 1558 she married the Dauphin who the following year was crowned as King Francis II of France. At sixteen years of age Mary Stuart was the Queen of France and Scotland, as well as the heir to the throne of Anglican England given that her cousin Elizabeth was childless. However, a widow at eighteen, she left her mother-in-law Catherine De Medici in order to return to her homeland, a Catholic Queen in a now Protestant country.

With the exception of the inhabitants of the Highlands, the doctrines of the Protestant preacher John Knox had opened a breach in the spirit of the Scots. Charismatic and sophisticated, the young sovereign found herself at the center of political intrigues and religious power struggles. The Puritans never forgave her joie de vivre, the luxury with which she surrounded herself and her many love affairs.

34 top *A view from above of Holyrood Palace and the ruins of the abbey that, legend has it, was founded in 1128 by David I, the son of Malcom III and Margaret. One day, while out hunting, the king was dismounted and wounded by a stag but was saved by his crucifix. He gave thanks by constructing the abbey. The name Holyrood derives from the words Holy and Rood, a synonym of cross.*

34-35 Holyrood Palace was built as a lodge for the abbey's guests and from the 16th century was developed into a royal residence. The lodge was made more comfortable by James IV. In 1529 the northwest tower was built to house the royal family. This is now the oldest surviving part of the palace and was the scene of many tumultuous scenes in the life of Mary Stuart: Mary married Lord Darnley in the abbey and Bothwell in what is today the Picture Gallery.

35 top left The oldest part of the castle, the Historical Apartments, are closely tied to the history of Scotland and Mary Queen of Scots. On the first floor of the tower are the two rooms in which the queen lived and which were the scene of the brutal assassination of Davide Rizzio. The embroidery work completed by Mary during her long imprisonment in England is exhibited in a display case.

35 bottom left At the center of the large square that extends in front of the entrance to the palace stands a fountain, a 19th-century copy of the one built at Linlithgow on the occasion of the marriage of James V and Mary of Guise, the parents of Mary Queen of Scots. On the occasion of the wedding wine rather than water flowed from the spouts.

35 right The statue of the unicorn stands out on the pilasters of the gateway to Holyrood House.

Mary established her court at Holyrood Palace in Edinburgh. Built in the twelfth century as an abbey, it was transformed into a royal residence by James IV, determined to make Edinburgh the center of his kingdom. The royal apartments, decorated in the Renaissance style and richly furnished, are still today the residence of Queen Elizabeth II and Prince Philip during their visits to the city. Thanks to a pa-

pal disposition Mary Stuart married her cousin Henry Darnley in 1565. The ceremony was followed by three days of dancing and banqueting. The royal couple's chambers can still be seen in the palace, including the room in which the queen met her enemy John Knox and the one in which she spent the afternoons playing the harp, writing poetry or listening to her secretary, and perhaps her lover, Davide Rizzio from Turin. The liaison between Mary and the Italian came to a tragic end. One evening, when the Queen was in the sixth month of her pregnancy, a group of armed men sent by Darnley attacked Rizzio, who vainly tried to defend himself by clinging to the Queen. He was finished off with stab wounds, but not before having crossed the royal bedchamber dripping blood.

Holyrood Palace is also the starting point of the Royal Mile, the road that, lined by towering grey façades, climbs the hill to Edinburgh Castle. Mary took this road in the tumultuous days following the assassination of Rizzio in order to seek refuge behind the powerful walls of the castle. The symbol of Scotland is stern and apparently invincible, even though it was actually conquered on a number of occasions by the English. The oldest

part of the complex is St. Margaret's Chapel, a stone building probably constructed at the behest of King David I in memory of his mother around 1130. Little remains of the ancient fortifications as they were incorporated into the extensions of the sixteenth and eighteenth centuries. The Royal Palace, the old Parliament Hall and the National War Memorial to those who fell during the Great War all overlook the interior courtyard, Crown Square. From the 16th century onwards the royal family preferred to live in more comfortable accommodation such as the palaces of Holyrood, Linlithgow and Falkland. The castle thus became the seat of government and a general military headquarter. Mary gave birth to the heir to the throne, the future James VI of Scotland, who became also James I of England after the death of Elizabeth I, in a small room on the 19th of June, 1566. She lowered the baby in a basket from a window so as to remove him from the danger of possible plots, the situation had precipitated. A plot in which Mary herself may have been involved, resulted in her second husband, Lord Darnley, being strangled. His remains were found in a building destroyed by an explosion. Three months later, to widespread disapproval, the Queen married the principal suspect of her husband's murder, James Hepburn, the Earl of Bothwell, who in the meantime had been cleared by the judges.

38 top left
The massive ruins of
Hermitage Castle rise
isolated by a torrent on
the remote moors of
Liddesdale, to the
north of Newcastleton.
Founded in the 13th
century, the castle was
rebuilt 200 years later
in an austere and

turreted style. Its
fame is linked with
the story of the Earl of
Bothwell and Mary
Stuart who, in order
to visit her beloved
wounded in a
skirmish on the
nearby border, did
not hesitate to ride 80
miles on horseback.

The marriage, celebrated in 1567 according to the Protestant rite, was the last straw for the Scottish noblemen, who attacked the couple. The queen managed to gather troops loyal to the crown and faced the rebels at Carberry Hill near Edinburgh. After a day of heated exchanges, Mary surrendered. Isolated and rejected as a sovereign, she was imprisoned in the fourteenth-century castle of Loch Leven, today in ruins, which was built on an island in the middle of the loch. The young queen remained a prisoner for almost a year, during which time she lost the twins she was carrying, but succeeded in escaping by boat, dressed as a peasant woman after having seduced Willie Douglas, the son of the Lord of the castle. An army of six thousand men loyal to the Queen engaged in battle with the anti-Catholic faction that supported the year-old King James VI at Langside near Glasgow. They were defeated and Mary Stuart fled southwards. She spent her last night in Scotland at Dundrennan Abbey before crossing the Solway Firth and seeking the help of her cousin Elizabeth I of England. Rather than receiving support, she was imprisoned for nearly twenty years in the Tower of London before being executed in 1587.

During the seven years of her reign, Mary Stuart visited most of Scotland, staying in castles that are still associated with her name. One of the most celebrated is Hermitage Castle, a massive stone building standing isolated on the moors bordering England, where Earl Bothwell, not yet her third husband, was wounded in a skirmish. From Jedburgh, to where she had gone to superintend the hearings of the Court of Justice, the sovereign rode to her lover's aid. During the return journey she fell from her horse and lay in a coma for some days in a tower house at Jedburgh. Craigmillar Castle, one of the Queen's favorite residences, stands not far from Edinburgh. The assassination of her second husband was apparently ordered in the massive sixteenth-century central tower surrounded by two curtain walls.

38 bottom left Just
a few miles separate
Edinburgh and
Craigmillar Castles,
the latter being a
brick tower with an
impressive curtain
wall raised in the
15th century, with
additions being made
over the following
centuries. This castle
was one of Mary
Stuart's favorites and
the area around it is
still known as Little
France after the
French servants of
Mary's court. It
would appear that it
was within these walls
that the plot against
Lord Darnley, Mary's
second husband, was
hatched.

38 top right
Borthwick Castle,
near Edinburgh, was
built in 1430 by the
1st Lord Borthwick
and is one of the most
powerful fortified
structures in
Scotland. Mary
Stuart visited the
castle in 1567, shortly
after her marriage
to Bothwell.

38-39 *Castle Campbell stands on a rocky crag in the heart of the wooded Ochil Hills. Dating from the 15th century, this tower house was the property of Colin Campbell, the 1st Earl of Argyll and chancellor of Scotland during the early years of the reign of James IV. In 1566 the castle was visited by the reformist preacher John Knox, Mary Stuart's great adversary. The Queen herself visited the castle in 1563. In 1645 it was conquered and burned by the Marquis of Montrose. A building in the French Renaissance style is linked to the castle.*

39 top *Loch Leven Castle stands on an island in a small lake at the southernmost tip of Perthshire. With its massive tower and curtain wall, it was used as an escape-proof prison from the 16th century. Mary Queen of Scots was imprisoned here for almost a year in 1567.*

40 top and 40-41 Falkland Palace rises at the foot of the gentle Lomond Hills in the heart of the rich Fife Peninsula. Between 1453 and 1463 James II and Mary of Guiderdal transformed the ancient fortress into a royal palace. The current appearance of the palace dates from the 16th century and was the work of the French and Scottish master masons working for James IV and James V, respectively the grandfather and father of Mary Queen of Scots. The palace is closely associated with the life of the tragic queen. In 1542, in fact, when Mary was just a few days old, her father James V died of a heart attack.

No trace remains, however, of Dunbar Castle to where the queen fled with Lord Darnley following the assassination of Rizzio and to where she returned a few months later on her honeymoon with Bothwell. Razed to the ground by her enemies following the Battle of Carberry Hill, it was definitively destroyed by Cromwell.

Mary spent what were perhaps the happiest days of her tormented life far from the intrigues of Edinburgh in Falkland Palace, the Stuart's favorite house. Originally built as a hunting lodge, the palace was enlarged by James IV who established an elegant court there. In preparation for his marriage to the daughter of the King of France, James V transformed Falkland into a Renaissance palace with the help of master craftsmen summoned from France. The palace is set in extensive grounds that also contain the world's first tennis court.

41 left and top right
The coat of arms of the Stuarts of Bute decorates the façade of the guardhouse that defended the entrance to Falkland Palace. It housed the private apartments of Keeper, the constable and guardian of the royal palace. The 3rd Earl of Bute acquired the palace and the title of Keeper in 1887. Lord Bute undertook a restoration project that was completed in 1900.

41 bottom right
The royal borough of Falkland around the royal castle is composed of a few simple, single story stone houses. The Bruce Fountain in stone with four bright red lions stands in the square at the end of Main Street, in front of the church and the two halls designed by Thomas Barclay and built between 1800 and 1801.

42 top The Keeper's Bedroom on the second floor of the palace, was used by Michael Crichton Stuart and his wife Barbara when, at the end of the 2nd World War, they transformed Falkland Palace into their home. The bedroom is dominated by a four-poster bed that is said to have belonged to James VI. Superbly figured, it dates from the 17th century.

42 bottom Completely rebuilt by Lord Bute, the Drawing Room is welcoming but simple, in line with the austerity of the post-war period when it was used by Michael Crichton Stuart and his wife Barbara who was responsible for the draperies. There are portraits of James V and his second wife Mary of Lorraine, James VI, Mary Queen of Scots, Anne of Denmark, Charles II and Catherine of Braganza.

42-43 The Old Library at Falkland Palace has an elaborate ceiling with trompe l'oeil decoration dating from 1895. The room was used as a study by Michael Crichton Stuart. On the walls are a royal hunting trophy and portraits of the family, including engravings of the 3rd Earl of Bute, Prime Minister George III and the great-grandfather of the 3rd Marquis.

43 top left During the brief years of her reign, Mary Stuart initiated work on the palace and its furnishings. Like her father and her grandfather, the queen loved to escape from the oppressive atmosphere of Edinburgh, made all the more intolerable by the austerity of the Reformation, to the tranquility of Falkland. In 1562, shortly after her return from France, the queen washed the feet of 19 virgins in Falkland Chapel, a number corresponding to the years of her reign.

43 top right The Tapestry Gallery linked the royal apartments with the Chapel and the keeper's apartments. Lord Bute restored the corridor and added the oak ceiling. The gallery is covered with 17th-century Flemish tapestries acquired in Holland, that were exposed when the royal family was living in the palace.

44 top The residence of the Roxburghe family, Floors Castle is surrounded by an agricultural estate extending over 56,000 acres along the banks of the River Tweed. The estate is composed of 50 tenanted farms, two grouse moors, 3900 acres of woodland, a golf course, a thoroughbred stud farm and salmon fishing reserves.

44-45 Built on a cliff dropping sheer to the sea, Tantallon Castle was considered to be impregnable as it was protected from attack by land by a double moat. Direct attacks and even incendiary arrows in fact failed to conquer the castle and it surrendered only in 1661 after 12 days of bombardment by Cromwell's troops under the leadership of General Monk.

S outhern Scotland is a region of golden hills, fields bordered by high hedges, stately homes and ruined abbeys, but also of forests and bleak heather-covered hills recalling those of the Highlands. The areas bordering England, to the south of the Scottish capital of Edinburgh, rarely enjoyed long periods of tranquility. From the incursions of the Roman legions until the Act of Union, the valley of the River Tweed and the Pentland and Moorfoot Hills were the theaters of savage and bloody battles. One of the most disastrous was the Battle of Flodden Field of 1513 in which the Scots were routed by the English army and James IV was killed. The Scottish king's year-old son succeeded him as James V, the future father of Mary Queen of Scots. In these turbulent lands, the castles represented the Scots' defensive kingpins. In the city of Harwick, close to the border, are the remains of one of the country's oldest defensive structures: an artificially raised earth mound that was once protected by palisades and on which stood a wooden lookout and defensive tower. At the foot of the tower a palisade protected houses and their inhabitants. No trace of the tower remains, but the Motte, the artificial mound, is still today the focal point of the Common Ridings, the costumed reconstructions that commemorate the site's tumultuous history. The ruins of Tantallon Castle standing above a rocky cliff at the mouth of the Firth of Forth are some of the most evocative in the whole of Scotland.

45 top The present-day appearance of Abbotsford, the home of Sir Walter Scott, dates from 1853 when the West Wing with the chapel, the kitchen and the servants' quarters was added. When Scott was alive he received in this house Maria Edgeworth, Wordsworth, Thomas Moore and Washington Irving. After the writer's death Queen Victoria visited Abbotsford and took tea with the family.

45 bottom The west façade of Hopetoun House overlooks the great park on the shores of the Firth of Forth, criss-crossed by nature trails open to the public. The hand of the architect William Bruce can be seen in the linearity of the façade.

46 top and 46-47 Set close to Edinburgh, Dalmeny House is the Gothic Revival home of the Earls of Rosebery and is filled with French furniture and paintings by Gainsborough, Reynolds and Lawrence. The house stands in extensive grounds that reach the seashore and within which pheasants with beautiful colored plumage wander undisturbed and sheep graze on the roadsides.

47 The home of the Hay family since 1696, Duns Castle stands in the southern part of the Borders region. The current owner has restored the castle to make it more comfortable without altering the characteristics of its rich past. The lake and grounds are particularly fine. The photos show the dining room and a detail of the exterior.

Built in the fourteenth century by the Douglas family in red sandstone, Tantallon was the last Medieval castle with curtain walls and an entrance tower to be constructed in Scotland. The austere and isolated Traquair House standing in the Tweed Valley is even older and its history is linked with that of Mary Queen of Scots and Bonnie Prince Charlie. In spite of its position close to the border and the unwavering devotion of its owners to the Stuarts, the castle has survived to the threshold of the new millennium virtually intact. The estate is still inhabited by the original owners who belong to a branch of the Stuart family. Thirlestane is another castle still inhabited by its owners, although its Medieval core has been extended and rebuilt over the centuries. At the end of the eighteenth century, following the Union with England, the region settled into a period of prosperity. The economic well-being resulting from the nascent industries led to a flourishing of the arts, architecture and literature. The area's most famous figures were no longer the representatives of the old aristocracy, but rather architects such as William and Robert Adam and poets and writers such as Robert Burns and Walter Scott. Edinburgh became a center of the arts and expanded with fine new quarters constructed in the Georgian style. The great Borders and Lothian estates also saw the construction of numerous mansions surrounded by parks and gardens. Among the most important were Hopetoun House on the western edge of Edin-

burgh and Mellerstain House, set between the River Tweed and the Cheviot Hills. Both were fruit of the Adam family genius. The initial designs by William Adam were subsequently developed by his sons, in particular Robert. William Adam was also responsible for the original design of Floors Castle, located close to the town of Kelso, amplified a century later by the architect Playfair. Floors Castle is today the largest inhabited castle in Scotland and was chosen as a location for the film *Greystoke*, in which it was the home of Tarzan. The revival of the legends of the Highlands influenced the country houses constructed by the great landowners of the Lowlands during the last century such as Dalmeny House, overlooking the Firth of Forth, or Abbotsford House, the beloved home of Sir Walter Scott, the writer and creator of the myth of romantic Scotland.

Surrounded by a large park on the South bank of the Firth of Forth, just a few miles out of Edinburgh, Hopetoun House was originally built by Sir William Bruce, the architect of Holyrood Palace, for the 1st Earl of Hopetoun, Charles Hope. The estate had been acquired in 1678 by his father John Hope, a descendant of a family of traders and judges. Unfortunately, John was never

able to live on the new property as he died in a shipwreck while accompanying the Duke of York, the future James VII of Scotland (James II of England). Work on the house began in 1699 with the construction of a central body that was extended in 1712 by William Adam and, following his death in 1748, by his three sons, John, Robert and James who were responsible for the decoration of the interiors between 1752 and 1767. The result is highly effective even though the hands of the different architects can be detected. The western façade with the classical central body is the work of Bruce. In contrast, the eastern façade, with the curving colonnades linking the wings to the central body is a theatrical stroke of genius by William Adam, undoubtedly one of his masterpieces. Inside the house, the staircases and the wooden paneling with inlaid flowers and fruits are by Bruce, while the salons with their stuccoed and gilded ceilings display the neo-classical touch of the Adams. Paintings by artists of the caliber of Rubens, Titian and Canaletto can be seen throughout the house, acquired by members of the family during the frequent foreign trips customarily taken in the last centuries by young members of the noble families. The opulent house was not inhabited throughout the year, however. The members of the family would spend weeks at the spa in Bath or would stay London while they enjoyed court life when they were not traveling in the direction of Paris or Rome.

48 top The Red Drawing Room is the only room in the house to retain its original function. The gilded stucco work of the ceiling is one of the most magnificent examples of Rococo decoration in Scotland and was the work of John Dawson. The red damask wallpaper dates from 1766. The furniture was made to measure to be set against the walls. In the 18th century, in fact, the room was used for entertaining. Only occasionally were small tables placed in the room. The white marble Italian fireplace features neo-classical decoration. The sofas and armchairs are upholstered in red damask.

48 bottom The staircase is undoubtedly the principal feature of the house designed by Bruce. The pine panels are carved with floral and fruit motifs, the work of Alexander Eizat who had already worked with Bruce at Holyrood Palace. The banister rail is carved from oak. On the walls hang the paintings commissioned to William McLaren in 1967 by the 3rd Marquis of Linlithgow in memory of his wife.

48-49 and 49 top *The western façade of the Georgian house is reflected in the waters of the lake. The grounds offer broad views of the shore of the Firth of Forth and the hills of the Fife peninsula. In early spring the grounds are ablaze with thousands of daffodils followed by primroses, bluebells and, in early summer by rhododendrons and azaleas. The extent of the park can be appreciated in the aerial view (top).*

50 top left
Sir William Bruce designed this bedroom for the young 1st Duke. It is composed of a series of three chambers including a dressing room and wardrobe. The wall covering with gilded decorations is the work of James Norrie of Edinburgh.

50 bottom left
The oak panels of this bedroom have led to it becoming known as the Wainscot Bed Chamber. The decoration dates from the early 17th century, with a series of wallpapers from Antwerp datable to the same period.

50 center right
The current Great Library is composed of numerous small, inter-connecting rooms that were originally used as bedrooms or writing rooms. The rebuilding and redesignation of the rooms was the work of Adam in 1720.

The library features books collected by the family with works on archaeology, law, philosophy, religion and European history. The environment is austere but very welcoming with the walls fully lined with wood and perfectly preserved books.

50 top right
The Yellow Drawing Room occupies the original dining room. The stucco-work on the ceiling is by John Dawson and the door and window frames

are by John Paterson, while the furniture in the Rococo style is by James Cullen. The yellow damask silk covering the walls is the original 1850 covering.

John MacKay, in his *Journey Through Scotland* published in 1728, writes, "The attractive palace and gardens are set in a great park, full of deer and surrounded by a stone walls. To the south of the main road there is the vegetable garden and close by the lodge for pheasants. Below the Earl's great terrace there is an oyster farm so that the kitchen can be supplied in great quantities throughout the year." On the 29th of August, 1822, Sir John Hope, the 4th Earl of Hopetoun, welcomed George IV to his home during his visit to Scotland, the first sovereign to set foot in the country after Charles II. The road from South Queensferry was completely repaved for the occasion and the gates of Hopetoun were opened to allow the people to see the king.

The Hope family created a charitable trust in 1974 to ensure the preservation of Hopetoun House, opening the main rooms to the public and reserving a wing of the house for themselves. During the summer months the house provides a magnificent setting for recitals of classical music.

50 bottom right The service room was created at the same time as the State Dining Room while a large kitchen was fitted out on the floor below. This photo shows

the system of bells used to call servants from the various rooms. Hot dishes were carried from the kitchen to the dining room in a steam-heated container.

51 The State Dining Room was designed in the 19th century by the architect James Gillespie Graham. It is a sophisticated and thorough example of the late period Regency style with original decor and furnishings such as the gilded stucco work of the frieze, the large

rayed medallion of the chandelier, the fireplace, the gold wall coverings and the elaborate drapes. The great mahogany table dates from 1820. There are numerous paintings on the wall including a portrait of the Countess of Hopetoun by Gainsborough.

THIRLESTANE CASTLE

The ancient royal village of Lauder, to the South of Edinburgh, is famous for hosting one of the oldest Common Ridings, the historical reconstructions of the cavalry skirmishes that took place throughout the Borders region. Thirlestane Castle stands on the bank of the River Leader and has been the home of the Maitland family from the sixteenth century to the present day. The castle boasts the most imposing and diversified façade of any in Scotland, with a host of symmetrical round or square towers and turrets, topped by parapets or pinnacles. The original tower, incorporated into the present building in pinkish stone with grey slate roofs, dates back to 1225. It was transformed into a residence by William, the secretary of Mary Queen of Scots. His brother John, the 1st Duke of Maitland, secretary and Chancellor to James VI, transformed it into a luxurious home with an oblong structure in red stone and a circular tower at each corner. A century later his grandson, the Duke of Lauderdale whose ghost is said to still haunt the castle, worked on the extension of Thirlestane with the royal architect Sir William Bruce, responsible for the rebuilding of Holyrood Palace in Edinburgh. Bruce added two massive square towers to which David Bryce in turn added two wings in dark stone during the last century. The interiors were renewed during the Victorian period, preserving the ceilings decorated with stucco-work from the sixteenth century. The castle also features the attractive old kitchens, and a nursery with a collection of antique toys including model soldiers, puppets, dolls, rocking horses and dolls' houses. The Borders Country Life Museum deals with the domestic life, agriculture and sport of the past centuries.

52 top right In 1840 the castle's kitchen was incorporated into the new South Wing where it continued to operate as we see it today until the end of the Second World War. The center of the room is dominated by the great work table. A laundry was created in the adjacent rooms.

52-53 The complex façade of Thirlestane Castle, the result of successive extensions, appears in all its beauty in the light of the sun that emphasizes the different color of the stone and accentuates the movement of the structure dominated by the tall central tower.

54 top left The magnificent portrait of Lady Grisell Hume, the wife of George Baillie, by Maria Varelst. Lady Grisell is the most important figure in the history of Mellerstain. When she was a girl of just twelve years of age she carried secret messages written by her father Sir Patrick Hume to his friend Baillie who was imprisoned in the Tolbooth in Edinburgh.

54 top right and 54-
55 The terraced
gardens on the south
side of the building
provide panoramic
views of the Cheviot
Hills and the lake, the
habitat of swans,
Canadian geese and

other wild birds. The
lake was originally
designed by George
Baillie, after his exile
in the Low Countries,
on the model of the
Dutch canals, and
then it was successively
extended.

MELLERSTAIN HOUSE

*55 top The small
drawing room presents
an intimate and
informal atmosphere,
with a Gothic touch in
the stucco-work of the
ceiling. Above the
Robert Adam fireplace
hangs a richly decorated
mirror.*

*55 center The Music
Room is a fine example
of Robert Adam's
versatility. The ceiling,
decorated with eagles
and sphinxes, still
features the colors
applied in 1773.
The mirrors were also
designed by Adam.
The portrait above the
fireplace by William
Aikman depicts Patrick
Hume, the 1st Duke of
Marchmont and father
of Grisell Hume. On
either side of the
fireplace hang portraits
by Maria Vareslet
depicting Lady Grisell's
daughters, Lady
Murray and Lady
Binning.*

*55 bottom
The Drawing Room
features a stuccoed
ceiling with the
original color scheme
specified by Robert
Adam in 1778.
He also designed the
fireplace with the two
lateral tables. Above
the fireplace hangs a
portrait of Isabella
d'Este from the School
of Parmegianino. The
sumptuous Napoleon
III-style carpet comes
from Aubusson.*

This large Georgian house is another of the Scottish masterpieces by the Adam architects, and it can be considered as a symbol of the architectural canons of the era: first and foremost the integration of architecture and natural beauty. The austere lines of the façade thus echo those of the Italianate garden with its terraces that descend towards the lake and the slopes of the Cheviot Hills in the background. The principal entrance overlooks green lawns, shrubs and low trees that grow denser as they approach the edge of the woods. Mellerstain House was constructed in two phases. The first two low wings with the tranquil charm of country cottages were designed by William Adam in 1725. The broad central block was completed forty-five years later, between 1770 and 1778, by his son, the famous architect Robert Adam: austere Gothic lines, yellow stone and battlements as the only concession to decoration. The house was built for the Baillies of Jerviswood, descendants of the rich Edinburgh merchant George Baillie who had bought the estate in 1742 and who had lived until his death in a large old house called Whiteside that stood not far from the present Mellerstain House. Many years were to pass before his grandson, who was also called George, after years of exile in Holland and economic privations, managed to return to his homeland in the retinue of the Prince of Orange, King William III.

56 top Luminous and welcoming, the small library occupies chambers that were originally designed as dressing rooms. The decor is the work of Robert Adam and dates from 1778. Among the pictures hanging on the walls is a portrait of Thomas, 6th Duke of Haddington by Sir Godfrey Kneller.

56-57 The library is full of classical references, beginning with the four long panels placed above the bookshelves with figures in white stucco against a dark green background. The scenes depict classical motifs such as the Nine Muses, the Sacrifice of Iphigenia, the Labors of Hercules and the Pleading of Priam for the Body of Hector.

57 top The Great Gallery is a long room that houses a small museum with objects collected by the family over the last two centuries. The ceiling was designed by Robert Adam, but never completed. Among the paintings on the wall is The Burgomaster Le Blom of Antwerp attributed to Van Dyck.

57 bottom The Stone Hall features a William Adam fireplace with precious Delft ceramic tiles. The landscape above the fireplace depicts the River Tweed at Kelso and was painted by R. Norrie in 1725. The round table dates from the Victorian period. Helmets and halberds complete the furnishings.

The Mellerstain estate was restored to its rightful owner and work began on the construction of a new house built to the designs of William Adam. George Baillie's wife, Lady Grisell Hume, became a legendary figure and her *Household Book* is considered a classic text providing insights into the social life of the era. On her death it was another grandson, George Haddington Baillie, who was responsible for completing the construction as we see it today.

Inspired by the classical architecture he had seen while on the Grand Tour through Greece and Italy he chose Robert Adam as his architect. The hand of the maestro is evident in the decoration of the elegant interiors which still today retain their original pastel colors and the ceilings decorated with stucco-work and medallions. The high point is the library with a play of pastel colors (pale green, pink, a bluish grey and ivory) in which the stucco decorations, the medallions, the bookshelves and the panels with classical figures are inserted. On the second floor is another of Adam's masterpieces, the Great Gallery with its Ionic columns. In this case, however, the ceiling was never finished. It remains a mystery as to what such a vast and sumptuous room in such an isolated part of the house was intended to be used as. It can only be reached via a secondary staircase and through a salon in the Oriental style. Mellerstain House also boasts a fine collection of antique furniture and paintings, among which is a Van Dyck.

FLOORS CASTLE

58 top Floors Castle is
surrounded by gardens
and a park designed
by William Adam.
However, prior to the
transformation of the
house, the formal
gardens were also
extended, being
transformed into an
open park reaching
the bank of the River
Tweed.

58-59 On the north
side can still be seen
the original central
body designed by
William Adam, to
which were added
the lateral towers
and the two wings
which repeat to a
smaller scale the
symmetrical design
of the central
element.

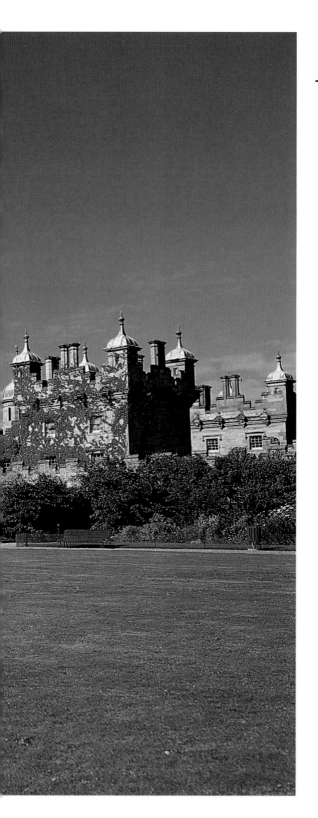

*F*loors Castle, set on a natural terrace at the foot of the Cheviot Hills, stands at the center of an estate in the Tweed valley, a few miles from the town of Kelso. Work on its construction began in 1721 at the behest of John, the 1st Duke of Roxburghe, an active promoter of the Act of Union, who commissioned William Adam to enlarge the earlier fortified castle and to create a residence in the Georgian style. All that remains of the great architect's design is a painting by William Wilson hanging in the sitting room.

James, the 6th Duke, had Adam's building "embellished" and in 1849 the architect William Playfair gave free reign to his imagination and talent, adding such a quantity of turrets, spires and cupolas as to make the castle resemble, according to a comment by Sir Walter Scott, that of Oberon and Titiana, the king and queen in Shakespeare's *Midsummer Night's Dream*. Early this century, thanks to the marriage of the 8th Duke to a rich American heiress, May Goelets, Floors Castle was endowed with an important art collection.

In the 1930s diverse modifications were made to the interior, in particular to the sitting room and the ballroom which were completely refurbished in order to exhibit the Brussels and Gobelins tapestries.

59 top The entrance hall is dominated by the portrait of the 3rd Duke painted in Rome by Pompeo Batoni in 1761-1762. Above the fireplace there is a large painting by Hendrick Danckerts that shows Charles II strolling with his court in Horse Guards Parade. In the background can be seen Whitehall. At the center of the room stands an oak table with lion's paw feet.

59 bottom This attractive room was refurnished by Duchess May in 1930 to make it less formal. On the walls can be seen a recent portrait of the present Duke by Howard Morgan, and a painting of Floors Castle in the design by William Adam. There is a small water-color of Kelso signed by Turner on the small table alongside the fireplace.

60 The great ballroom was designed by Playfair in 1842 and enjoys a broad view over the river. In the 1930s Duchess May covered the 19th-century decorations with oak panels on which hang 18th-century Gobelins tapestries depicting Neptune, Ceres, Venus, Cupid and Juno.

61 Designed as a billiards room by the architect Playfair, this room was subsequently converted into a dining room. It today houses a rich collection of silverware, including the cutlery created by Paul Stort in 1819 and the cups with gilded silver handles made by Paul de Lamerie in 1726. Among the portraits hanging on the walls is one of the actress Peg Woffington by Hogarth.

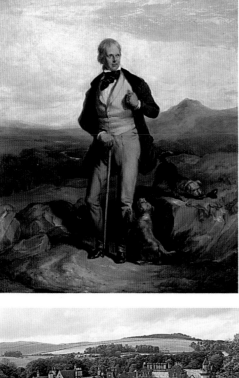

The valley of the River Tweed was the area of Scotland beloved of Sir Walter Scott, the writer whose novels contributed to the nineteenth-century fashion for romantic Scotland and to the revival of bagpipes and kilts that had been virtually abandoned following the defeat at Culloden. He had been aware of the beauty of the region ever since his childhood spent on his grandfather's farm at Sandyknowe close to Mellerstain House. When, in 1799, he was appointed Sheriff of Selkirk he was able to settle definitively in the Borders. In 1812 he acquired Cartleyhole Farm where he began work on a series of new novels including *Waverley* and *Rob Roy*. Ten years later he demolished the old farmhouse and began work on Abbotsford House, so named in commemoration of the fact that the land had once belonged to the wealthy Melrose Abbey. The new building with its turrets and battlements was designed by William Atkinson in imitation of a Scottish baronial castle of the previous centuries. Typically, Scott turned the house into a concentration of elements symbolizing Scottish Romanticism, from the sword said to have belonged to the outlaw hero Rob Roy MacGregor to a reproduction of the portal of the nearby abbey. In the library, a large room overlooking the river, the walls are lined with the 9000 volumes collected by the writer, while the ceiling is an exact replica of the one in the chapel at Rosslyn.

62 center and bottom Abbotsford House is a distillation of 19th-century Scottish Romanticism. A lover of the legendary past of Scotland, the writer was in fact proud of his homeland and an enthusiastic expert on the heroes of the Highlands such as Rob Roy or the glorious William Wallace, of whom he collected relics and mementoes.

62-63 Surrounded by greenery, Abbotsford House, seen in this aerial photo, is a triumph of Gothic Revival decoration. It houses the Scott Museum which recounts the life of the novelist and exhibits many of the objects he collected during his lifetime or received as gifts.

63 top In 1812 Sir Walter Scott moved with his family to Cartleyhole and between 1817 and 1821 extended the small farm until it reached the size of the present-day Abbotsford House, of which the façade overlooking the river can be seen here. In 1830, when the writer was declared bankrupt, his creditors allowed him to keep the estate.

64 top The library is the most beautiful room in Abbotsford House, overlooking the River Tweed. The over nine thousand volumes are arranged around the walls. Some of them carry the legend "Clausus Tutus Ero" engraved on the spine, an anagram of Gualterus Scotus. The ceiling was deliberately copied from the one destroyed in the Abbey at Rosslyn.

64-65 The entrance hall at Abbotsford is panelled in oak. Some of the panels are finely carved and came from the Auld Kirk in Dunfermline. Others actually came from Holyrood Palace. In this room one can also admire armor, helmets and other objects collected personally by Sir Walter Scott on the battlefield at Waterloo.

65 *top left Between the drawing room and the dining room lies the small armory which in Scott's day was used as a smokers' corridor and now contains a vast collection of pistols and swords, including a Highlands broad sword. Some of the objects are associated with Rob Roy, the legendary Scottish hero and protagonist in one of Scott's novels.*

65 *top right Sir Walter Scott died on the 21st of September, 1832, in the dining room, which is still used today for family meals. "It was such a quiet day, that the sound he loved most, the gentle murmur of the voice of the Tweed over its pebbles could clearly be heard while we were gathered around his bed," wrote his son-in-law Walter Lockhart.*

65 *center right Not accessible to the public, the private study is full of memories and relics of the family. The descendants of Sir Walter Scott still live in the 19th-century house although it has now been opened to the public.*

65 *bottom right Sir Walter Scott's writing desk was made as a copy of the one owned by his friend John Morrit using wood from a ship of the Spanish Armada. In this room the writer, who collected ancient Scottish poems and stories so as to rewrite them in the form of ballads and novels, produced some of his historical novels.*

TRAQUAIR HOUSE

Massive and imposing, with small windows and two low wings, Traquair House is the oldest continuously inhabited building in the whole of Scotland. Its origins are lost in the mists of the first millennium, although it is first documented in 1107 when it was used as a lodge by Alexander I when hunting in Ettrick Forest. Alexander was the first of a long line of Scottish kings who stayed at Traquair and it remained a royal residence until the thirteenth century. During the reign of David I, the successor to Alexander, local laws were proclaimed, justice was dispensed and assemblies of the clan chieftains were held at Traquair. Many of the Traquair Charters, such as those signed by King William the Lion which granted the status of city to Glasgow, are still preserved in the castle and are exhibited to the public in rotation in the museum room and the library. On the death of Alexander III in 1286 the oldest dynasty of Scottish kings was extinguished and the period of peace in the Borders was interrupted. During the war for independence Traquair became a strategic element in the defensive system thanks to its position on the riverbank. The course of the Tweed was actually diverted in the mid-seventeenth century by the first Earl of Traquair in order to prevent damp from undermining the foundations of the castle. Occupied by the English during the reigns of Edward I and II, the castle returned to Scottish hands thanks to Robert the Bruce. Then, for 150 years the property passed from one owner to another as the political climate shifted. When James III came to the throne in 1460 he granted Traquair to his favorite Robert Lord Boyd. In 1478 the uncle of the King, the Duke of Buchan, became the owner. It was then inherited by the Duke's brother James Stuart, an ancestor of the current owners. The Stuarts of Traquair supported Mary Queen of Scots and, subsequently, the Jacobite cause.

66 top and 66-67 Traquair House, the oldest inhabited house in Scotland, is surrounded by a luxuriant garden overlooking the River Tweed. During the religious wars a Catholic priest was concealed in the house in a secret room that can still be seen on the third floor, adjacent to the library where religious services were held.

66 bottom A soft rug, two sofas and an armchair in front of the fireplace lend the Lower Drawing Room a warm, welcoming atmosphere. The mirror above the fireplace and the paintings flanking it on the same wall are particularly fine.

67 top The High Drawing Room conserves a simple, tranquil appearance, with white sofas, doors and walls and a collection of portraits of women: Christian Anstruther, the wife of the 6th Earl of Traquair, Lady Isobel and Lady Jean Seton painted by Cornelius Jansen. Gilded panels and decorations are set above the doors and the fireplace. In a corner of the room is a harpsichord by Andreas Ruckers from 1651.

68 top left In large old houses such as Traquair, servants were often summoned by a complex system of bells connecting every room. Generally the bells were placed in a passageway between the kitchen and the pantry so that they could be heard by the entire staff.

68 top right Family portraits are hung on the walls of the sober dining room in the South Wing of the house. Set above the fireplace is a portrait of the 1st Earl of Traquair. On his left is the Jacobite 5th Earl, Charles. Among the women is the 4th Countess of Traquair.

68-69 Set on the third floor, the austere library dates from the middle of the 18th century. The walls are lined with antique and rare volumes. The painted frieze framing the ceiling features busts of major figures from antiquity.

69 top The old laundry is in reality a small museum of objects from the past, from old cast-iron flat-irons to coal scuttles. The most unusual piece is an old mangle from 1840, that was once used to smooth and iron the clothes.

69 center and bottom The royal bed chamber is dominated by a sumptuous yellow four-poster bed in which it is said that Mary Stuart once slept. Legend has it that the bedspread is the work of the queen and her ladies-in-waiting, the four Maries. It is also said

that the cradle was used for James VI, the future James I of England. The portrait close to the window is of Lady Ann Seton, the wife of the 2nd Earl of Traquair. The adjacent room is the dressing room with a bath and toilet necessities.

The castle thus became a haven for Catholic priests, as demonstrated by the priest's hole, accessed by a secret flight of steps.

In 1566 Mary Queen of Scots stayed at Traquair with Lord Darnley. A blanket embroidered by Mary and her ladies-in-waiting remains as evidence of her passing. The ceremonial entrance, the Bear Gate, named after the bears decorating the pilasters, has been locked since 1745 when the Earl of the day wished good luck to Bonnie Prince Charlie and swore that it would not be opened until the Stuarts had been returned to the throne.

The present appearance of Traquair House is the result of diverse transformations executed principally during the fifteenth and seventeenth centuries. The defensive tower of the ancient Scottish kings has been incorporated into the mansion house; in the mid-16th century a new wing was added with a rectangular tower protecting the West side, while another wing dates from the end of the seventeenth century.

Inside the house there are collections of ceramics and porcelain, portraits of local noblemen, the beds in which royalty slept during their stays and a beautiful library with a wealth of antique books which are not in the best of condition due to the damp. The chapel is decorated with wooden bas-reliefs from Flanders. The cellars house a collections of tools and the fascinating system of bells used to summon servants.

*70 top
The general symmetry of Drumlanrig Castle is also seen in the details such as the windows, the chimneys and the turrets. The fascinating 17th-century building in pink stone is surrounded by a large park delimited by the wild Dumfrieshire Hills.*

70-71 Built in 1270 and extended over the course of the centuries, Caerlaverock Castle features three corner towers, one of which has been completely destroyed. The entrance on the north side gives an impression of great solidity but the castle was nonetheless conquered by the English immediately after construction had been completed.

I rish monks brought Christianity to the land of the Picts and the Scots by way of this rugged coastline in which the border between lake and sea is uncertain. Tradition has it that they brought with them the Stone of Destiny which has ever since symbolized the power of the Crown and upon which the kings and queens of Great Britain are still crowned in Westminster Abbey. From the fifth century onwards the Celts joined forces with the local peoples to create the small kingdom of Dalriada. The royal capital was a fortress perched on the hill of Dunadd and surrounded by water and marshes. Today, on the crag that overlooks the wilderness of Crinan Moss, all that remains are ruined walls, a hollowed stone and a panel with inscriptions in *ogham*, the oldest form of Celtic writing, all symbols of the coronation ceremony. Tradition has it that in 574, St. Columba crowned King Aidan, perhaps the first Christian ceremony to be held in the British Isles. The raids of the Vikings and their settlement on the coast that so closely resembled their native fjords, slowly eroded the power of the tiny kingdom. The capital was moved to Dunstaffnage, to the North of Oban, where in 850 Kenneth MacAlpine took steps to fuse his kingdom with that of the Picts, transferring the court and the Stone of Destiny to Scone in Central Scotland. In 1060 with Malcom Canmore, the region became part of the Kingdom of Scotland al-

beit retaining a degree of independence thanks to the power of the local nobles. During the twelfth century a chieftain from Morven, Somerled, married the daughter of a Norwegian king thus obtaining vastly increased power and giving rise through his three descendants to the diverse branches of the MacDonald clan. Towards the end of the century the head of the Campbell clan was Cailen Mor of Loch Awe whose descendants became the dukes, earls and marquises of Argyll. The relative autonomy of the region with respects to the Crown continued until 1455 when James II took Threave Castle, the home of the Douglas clan, the Lords of Galloway. This five-story tower house was built on an island in the River Dee by the 3rd Earl of Douglas between 1369 and 1390. Dating from the late thirteenth century is Caerlaverock Castle, a fortress with an unusual triangular plan surrounded by a moat, austere on the outside but with an internal courtyard elegantly decorated with Renaissance motifs. Following the wars for independence there was a long period of internal conflict as the various clans struggled for power and land, at times supporting, at others rebelling against the Scottish Crown. The most tragically famous episode was that of the massacre of the Mac-Donalds by the Lords of Argyll, the Campbells. The government in England had set a date, the 31st of December, 1691, for the definitive submission of the clans to the Crown.

The MacDonalds of Glen Coe reached Fort William late and were unable to find the magistrate authorized to hear their oath of allegiance. They thus journeyed to Inveraray to swear the oath. The paperwork arrived in Edinburgh just a few days late but this was sufficient to provoke extremely severe punishment: on the 13th of February 1692 at Glen Coe over 200 persons were massacred including women, old people and children. The castle of the Dukes of Ar-

gyll, the leaders of the Campbell clan, is located at Inveraray and in its present form with turrets and false battlements dates from the eighteenth century. Culzean Castle, an elegant neo-classical mansion by Robert Adam overlooking the sea, dates from the same era and is surrounded by a large park. Another great Scottish ar-chitect, Sir William Bruce, was responsible for the design of Drumlanrig Castle, in the heart of Dumfries and Galloway, a region in the Southwest of Scotland. Brodick Castle on the island of Arran is the result of repeated and successive extensions, the last of which dates from the mid-Victorian period.

72 top Dunstaffnage Castle stands on a rocky promontory dominating Loch Etive. The current building dates from the 13th century and presents a powerful curtain wall and three defensive towers. In the mid-18th century it became the prison of Flora MacDonald, the woman from Skye who aided the escape of the unfortunate Bonnie Prince Charlie, the last of the Stuart dynasty to lay claim to the Scottish throne.

72 bottom Romantic
and imposing, in spite
of being partially
ruined, Threave
Castle is reached by
boat across the River
Dee. Following the

battle of Flodden
Field a defensive ring
with walls and towers
was added. Only the
bare walls remained
after the Covenanters'
siege of 1640.

72-73 Bothwell
Castle in Strathclyde
was fought over at
length during the
wars of
independence. Part
of the original

circular tower still
exists today, although
the majority of the
castle is the result of
additions made
during the 14th and
15th centuries.

INVERARAY CASTLE

75 right Halberds from the 16th and 17th centuries, Brown Bess muskets from 1740, axes from 1847 and 18th-century Scottish broadswords are exhibited in the armory. All of the arms are carefully displayed in a circular arrangement echoing the arches of the room. The display cases contain collections of Scottish daggers, powder flasks and the belt and dagger of Rob Roy.

74-75 In this aerial view Inveraray Castle appears in all its glory, made all the more romantic by the symmetry of the gardens and by the wild natural surroundings. The Gothic towers, the pinnacles and the eclecticism of the external decoration make it a true fairy-tale castle.

75 top left The tapestry gallery was furnished between 1780 and 1790 according to the sophisticated French taste with a rich collection of Beauvais tapestries made to measure for the castle. The richness of the room is enhanced by the stucco-work and the painted decoration by the artist Girard. The coat of arms of the 7th Duke and his third wife Anne Colquohon Cunningham is inlaid in the marble top of the small round table.

75 bottom left The Victorian bed chamber contains the maple wood writing desk presented by Queen Victoria to her daughter Louise on the occasion of her marriage to the future Duke of Argyll. Between the two windows can be seen a depiction of the wedding ceremony in the chapel at Windsor painted by Sydney Hall.

*I*nveraray is a village built during the eighteenth century on the shores of Loch Fyne, close to the mouth of the River Aray from which it takes its name. Developed on a cross-shaped plan, the castle is a perfect example of neo-classical architecture. It was commissioned by Archibald, the 3rd Duke of Argyll, who established an ambitious plan to replace the crumbling Medieval castle built in 1457 by his ancestor Colin. In order to create the new stately home and the grounds that were to surround it, the old village was demolished and completely rebuilt a short distance away. The work was completed between 1770 and 1780 in the face of myriad difficulties given that at that

time there were no viable roads within forty miles. The new residence of the Campbells, the Dukes of Argyll, one of Scotland's most powerful families who led the Covenanters during the religious wars of the mid-seventeenth century, was designed by the architect Roger Morris of the Palladian school. The symmetrical appearance of the building was, however, modified during the last century when, following a fire, the corner towers were capped and garrets were added, topped with minuscule tympanums in an incredible medley of styles. The resulting building features turrets like those of fairy-tale castles and magnificently decorated halls. The best of these is the great dining hall with colored ornamental motifs painted in 1784 by the French painters Girard and Gruinard.

76 One of a pair of geese from the Chinese Chi'en Lung dynasty (1736-1795) exhibited in the dining room. This goose is holding a fish in its beak, while its pair has an eel. The two ceramic sculptures were used as soup tureens. Along with the miniature cannon in embossed silver and gold they are among the rarest pieces in the castle.

Set between the peninsula of Kintyre and the West Coast, the small island of Arran is dominated by the peak of Goat Fell. At its foot, overlooking Brodick Bay, stands a romantic Victorian-looking ivy-covered castle built in red stone. Surrounded by luxuriant grounds, up until 1957 the castle was the home of the Dukes of Hamilton in which they studied, gardened and received guests in a very informal atmosphere. On the death of the last owner, Duchess Mary Louise of Montrose, the castle passed to the state and thence to the National Trust for Scotland. The castle was built in the thirteenth century on the ruins of an earlier Viking fortress. However, only parts of the base of this Medieval tower, once of strategic importance in the defence of the Clyde estuary, have survived.

76-77 and 77 top In the photo appears the avenue leading to Brodick Castle, an elegant Victorian manor house with ancient Medieval origins. Around the castle extends a large formal garden with flower beds and rhododendrons planted by the last Duchess of Montrose. In 1980 the woods of Brodick Castle became the first natural park in the Scottish islands managed by the Countryside Commission for Scotland. The woods are inhabited by squirrels, peregrine falcons and even the golden eagle.

78 bottom left The kitchen is large and airy, equipped with two hearths, three ovens and an original spit driven by a water wheel. Almost the entire battery of copper pans is original, with just a few pieces being added recently. Much of the pewter is stamped with the symbol of the Hamilton family.

78 top right The Drawing Room is the largest room in the castle and is located in the Victorian wing added in 1844. It contains a number of examples of superb craftsmanship from candelabras to ceramics, as well as a number of magnificent paintings including the portrait of the Duchess of Montrose by De Laszlo.

On the death of William, the 2nd Duke of Hamilton, at the Battle of Worcester, Cromwell's troops occupied the castle in 1652 and a new wing was added. In spite of the successive interventions, the castle was not inhabited by the family until the end of the last century when, on the crest of the wave of interest in the Highlands and attracted by the wealth of game, the Hamiltons decided not to develop the estate which actually represented a minor part of their patrimony centering on Hamilton Palace in Lanarkshire. In 1843 Alexander, the 10th Duke, commissioned an extension to the castle on the occasion of the marriage of his son William, the future 11th Duke, and the German princess Mary of Baden, a cousin of Napoleon. The design of the new wing, to the west of the old tower, was entrusted to James Gillespie Graham, one of the architects of Edinburgh's New Town. The result is a castle of baronial appearance in which the new elements fuse perfectly with the old and the linear design of the fenestration contrasts harmoniously with the battlements and the gargoyles of the roof. Gillespie was responsible for the entrance hall, dark and imposing, with arms and hunting trophies along with an oak fireplace inlaid with the family's coat of arms. The castle houses a rich collection of silver, porcelain and paintings, including works by Watteau and Turner, part of the remarkable collection of William Beckford, father-in-law of the 10th Duke. There is also an attractive library with equestrian prints on the walls, and a kitchen with an exceptional battery of copper pans. In the castle grounds, the walled garden dates from 1710, but the true masterpiece is the rhododendron garden established by the Countess of Montrose and considered to be one of the most beautiful anywhere in Great Britain with dozens and dozens of diverse varieties. There is also an interesting ice room that was packed with snow gathered from the mountains or imported from Canada during the winter to provide a year-round supply for the conservation of food before the introduction of refrigerators. In 1980, the woodlands on the estate were declared a Country Park with 10 miles of marked footpaths along the Hamilton and Montrose families' favorite walks.

78-79 Situated in the 16th-century wing, the dining room is a majestic and imposing space. The ceiling in white stucco dates from 1844, while the wood paneling which came from Letheringham Abbey in Suffolk was installed in 1920. Above the fireplace hangs a painting by Philip Reinagle depicting the struggle between William Warr and William Wood at Nevestock in 1788. Each year the table is laid according to a family tradition, using silverware and porcelain belonging to the Beckford and Hamilton collections.

79 top left The entrance hall was built in 1844 to the designs of the architect James Gillespie Graham. The coat of arms of the Duke of Hamilton is carved in oak above the fireplace. The furniture is mainly Victorian, although in some cases the wood used to make it came from the existing furnishings. A collection of hunting trophies is displayed in the hall and along the stairs, with 87 heads of deer hunted on the island. There is also a fine collection of sporting scenes by James Pollard.

79 top right
A portrait of the Duke of Alençon by François Clouet hanging in the drawing room. The work once belonged to Charles I as testified by the symbol on the back.

CULZEAN CASTLE

The windows look out onto the grey sea of the Firth of Clyde and the narrow strip of land called the Mull of Kintyre that ventures out into the ocean. Inside there is stucco-work, pastel colors and crystal chandeliers. It is in the salon of Culzean Castle on the Southwest Coast, a few miles from the celebrated Turnberry golf course, that the barren, romantic scenery of the region contrasts most magnificently with the elegance of the Georgian architecture and decoration of Robert Adam. The castle stands at the top of a cliff that drops sheer to the sea and is surrounded by the large estate inherited in 1744 by Sir Thomas Kennedy, the 9th Earl of Cassillis. The existing Medieval castle was composed of a round tower with a room on each floor, a purely defensive structure lacking any form of creature comfort. The Duke therefore decided in 1760 to add a long wing overlooking the sea. However, the new construction reflected his pragmatic spirit that was more interested in the modernization of the estate than in the elegance of his home. This situation changed seventeen years later when the Earl's brother David, the 10th Earl of Cassillis, called upon the most celebrated architect of the era, Robert Adam, to rebuild Culzean Castle and make it more suitable to the worldly lifestyle of the period.

80 top and center
The traditional home of the Kennedy family, Culzean Castle, inherited by the 9th Earl of Cassillis in 1744, immediately took the place of Dunure, the family's ancient castle. Robert Adam's design has a classical linearity that, however, does not disdain Medieval touches such as the slits and crenellated turrets.

80 bottom Culzean Castle is surrounded by extensive grounds transformed into a Country Park, and a large walled garden, the lake of swans and various buildings such as Camellia House. A group of naturalist guides is at the service of visitors to provide guided botanical tours. The park headquarters was opened in 1970 in the Robert Adam-designed Home Farm.

80-81 and 81 top Set in a spectacular position at the top of a cliff dropping sheer to the Firth of Clyde, Culzean Castle dominates the whole of the West Coast. The imposing but severe exterior is softened by the large green lawns, the flower beds and the terraces on which even tropical trees flourish.

The old building was demolished and replaced with a round tower that accentuated the romantic aura of the complex as a whole. Inside, on the first floor, Adam designed the stunning Saloon, a symbol of the elegance of the century, and dealt personally with every last detail of the furnishing. The interiors in fact constitute one of the last and most successful works of the architect and his team of artists and craftsmen who had already proven their talents at the houses of Hopetoun and Mellerstain near Edinburgh. The circular ceiling panels were painted by the Italian artist Antonio Zucchi, the marble fireplaces were the work of Peter Henderson of Edinburgh while the great round carpet was woven not far from Culzean to a specific design. Adam's masterpiece, though, is the oval staircase located in what was once a dark, cramped interior courtyard behind the tower. Sober and elegant, the staircase rises between two stories of Corinthian columns while the play of curved lines creates an impression of movement. When David Kennedy died in 1792 without heirs, Culzean Castle passed to his cousin, Captain Archibald Kennedy of New York whose home address was No. 1 Broadway. During the last century the symmetry of Adam's original design was lost with the construction of a new wing. In 1945, Charles Kennedy, the 14th Earl of Cassillis, presented the castle to the National Trust for Scotland on the condition that the upper floor was made available to General Eisenhower as a sign of the Scottish people's gratitude for his feats during the war. A great park extends around the castle in which woodland alternates with avenues of rhododendron and Italian gardens overlooking the sea. Artificial corridors link the fountain of the Court Garden to the large walled garden where the typically British art of contrasting flowers of various heights and colors is seen to best effect.

83 top left The dining room occupies what were originally the library and the master dressing room. Vast and imposing, it is dominated by a long 18th-century table and Chippendale-style chairs. The painting above the mantelpiece by Ben Marshall dates from 1800 and depicts the 12th Duke of Cassillis, subsequently nominated Marquis of Aisla.

83 top, right The oval staircase is one of Adam's masterpieces and one of the principal features of Culzean Castle. It has a double row of Corinthian columns on the first floor and Ionic on the second to accentuate the perspective. The stairs, together with the banister and the red carpet, create a contrast of colors and curving lines.

DRUMLANRIG CASTLE

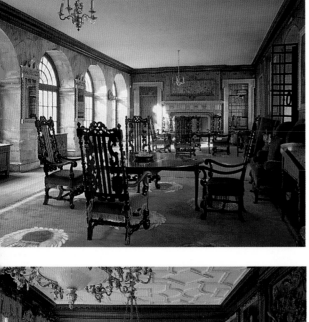

Drumlanrig Castle was originally built in the fourteenth century as a Douglas stronghold, but little trace of the early structure remains. The present castle with four corner towers was built by William Douglas, the 1st Duke of Queensberry in the decade between 1679 and 1691. It is the work of different architects, also Sir William Bruce is known to have worked on the plans, and the final result is a unique example of late seventeenth century Renaissance architecture in pink sandstone. When the castle was completed the Duke was so shocked by how much it had cost that he felt uneasy to live there. From an architectural point of view Drumlanrig constitutes the link between the fortresses built prior to the Act of Union and the "mock" castles constructed by the nobility as country houses. Drumlanrig has nothing of the Romantic fortified castles of other parts of Scotland. Its monumental appearance confers an air of great severity, unusual for a private home in the heart of the countryside. However, as soon as one enters the interior courtyard this austerity is mitigated. The entrance has a vaulted arch with Renaissance decoration and a Gothic structure supporting a terrace.

84 right The oak staircase and balustrade were among the first of their kind Scotland. That which in all the other Scottish castles is a simple passageway, at Drumlanrig takes on the role of a veritable art gallery with paintings of international importance from the Madonna with Yarnwinder *by Leonardo to the* Old Woman Reading *by Rembrandt along with other works by Hans Holbein, Murillo, Joost Van Cleef and a* Madonna *from the School of Correggio.*

84-85 and 85 top Drumlanrig Castle, a pink sandstone construction, stands on a hill (Drum) and the end of a long (lang) ridge (rig). Surrounded by woods, this castle is one of the first examples in Scotland of the Renaissance style applied to civic architecture. Among the guests to have stayed at Drumlanrig were James VI, Bonnie Prince Charlie, Queen Elizabeth II and Prince Philip and also Neil Armstrong, the first man to have set foot on the moon.

86 top At Kirkwall, the capital of the Orkney Islands, off the North coast of Scotland, stand the beautiful ruins of Earl Patrick's castle, begun in 1607 by Earl Patrick Stuart, the brother of Mary Stuart and the illegitimate son of James V.

THE HIGHLANDS

*I*nhabited ever since ancient times, as testified to by over 500 brochs, the defensive towers having been built 2000 years ago, the Highlands has not always been an immense pasture for millions of sheep. Once upon a time the northernmost region of Scotland, this harsh, beautiful land, was covered with forests and the cultivated fields of the Highlanders, peoples of Celtic origin who lived in agricultural communities, the clans, ever ready to go to war at the behest of their chieftains. One of the most powerful of these clans was that of the McLeods; descendants of the Vikings of the Isle of Man. Their castle was at Dunvengan, on the Isle of Skye. The Scandinavian blood was mixed with that of the Celts of the Kingdom of Alba and reinforced the powerful clan communities which frequently engaged in struggles amongst themselves. The chieftains lived in defensive towers such as those of Eilean Donan Castle, the home of the MacKenzies, or Cawdor Castle, the residence of the Thanes of Cawdor. At the end of the Stuart dynasty the Highlands witnessed repeated revolts against the ruling house of Hanover. The region's castles such as Blair or Braemar changed ownership on a number of occasions and in some cases were transformed into barracks for troops. In 1715 there was an unsuccessful revolt led by the Duke of Mar who intended to bring James Edward, the younger son of James I, to the throne. The Highlanders were defeated at Sheriffmuir and the British army constructed new roads from Crieff to Fort William in order to

keep the region under military control. Bonnie Prince Charlie returned from exile in France in 1745, landing in the Hebrides. He gathered all the clans faithful to the Stuarts at Glenfinnan and the following month entered Edinburgh, installing himself at Holyrood Palace. The rebel troops scored a victory at Prestonpans and advanced through the English Midlands as far as Derby. However, they were defeated at Culloden near Inverness in the April of 1746. Bonnie Prince Charlie had to flee and the repression of the Jacobites was ruthless. The survivors were forbidden to wear their kilts, to bear arms, to speak Gaelic and to play the bagpipes. The lands of the clan chieftains who had supported the Jacobites were confiscated and the clan system was dismantled. This marked the Highlanders' ruin. Accustomed for centuries to paying rent to the clan chieftain for their land in the form of military service, they were unable to find the money demanded by the new landowners. The English lords faithful to the Crown found it more convenient to transform their holdings into pasture or hunting estates. With the Highlands Clearances, the Highlanders were expelled from their lands, their houses were burned to prevent rebellions and any attempt at resistance was repressed. Many people emigrated and by 1860 the Highlands had been emptied. In the meantime, however, English society had developed a love of this wild and remote Scotland, so much so that Queen Victoria ordered the construction of Balmoral Castle, the royal family's current summer residence.

86-87 The dramatic ruins of Urquhart Castle stand on a promontory reaching out into Loch Ness. The castle, one of the largest in Scotland, fell into ruin after 1689. Most of what remains standing dates from the 16th century.

For centuries Dunrobin Castle has been the home of the Dukes of Sutherland, descendants of Freskin of Moravia who arrived in Scotland at the time of William the Lion. They immediately adopted the customs and culture of their new homeland, to the extent that they transformed themselves into Celtic chieftains and were invested in 1235 with the title of Earl of Sutherland. Their symbol, a Great Cat, led to the name Caithness, the northeastern region of the Highlands. Built on a terrace overlooking the sea, this castle with its turrets and pinnacles has no less than 187 rooms and is the largest home in northern Scotland. Dunrobin, whose name means the "Castle of Robin," is documented for the first time in 1401 as the fortress of the 6th Earl. However, there was also an older part, a Medieval tower dating from 1275, the remains of which can be seen in the windowed corridor. In the seventeenth century two wings were built to the south and the west to form an L-shaped plan. A wide tower with a circular plan united them to the Medieval fortress. In 1785 Elizabeth, the Countess of Sutherland, married Viscount Trentham, the Marquis of Stafford, an English noblemen and one of Europe's richest men thanks in part to the profits of the industrial revolution. A philanthropist with liberal ideas, he established large-scale programs for the improvement of the living conditions, the roads and the economy of the region.

88 top The elegant dining room was redesigned by Sir Robert Lorimer following the fire of 1915. The walls are fully paneled in wood and are topped with a classical frieze, probably of Italian origin. The room features a number of important family portraits. Above the fireplace Thomas Phillips has immortalized the sons of the 1st Duke; to the right is a portrait of Granville, the 1st Marquis of Stafford by George Romney and on the side wall, the Duchess Harriet, the wife of the 2nd Duke, with her eldest daughter, Elizabeth.

88 bottom This big silver cup occupies a first floor niche in one of the two turrets of Dunrobin Castle.

88-89 Overlooking the sea and surrounded by formal gardens of Franco-Scottish inspiration, Dunrobin Castle dates from the 13th century but was extended on more than one occasion from the 17th century onwards. The interiors feature furniture and paintings of great value as well as objects that recount the history of the family and Scotland itself.

89 top Seen from the terrace, the gardens of Dunrobin reveal the intricate design inspired by Versailles and the geometric pattern that develops around the fountain.

90 top The library has taken the place of a bedroom and related dressing room. Entirely lined with bookshelves, it is dominated by the fine portrait of Duchess Eileen, the wife of the

5th Duke, painted by Philip Lazlo. Apart from the ten thousand volumes, some of which are very rare, the library also contains a huge globe by W. & A. K. Johnstone.

90 bottom The nursery contains toys used by the young Sutherlands over the centuries. In the foreground stands a wooden rocking horse while in the background there is a Victorian dolls' house.

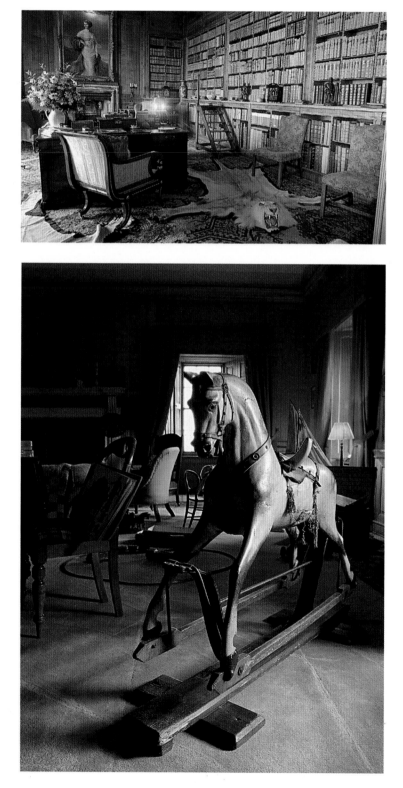

On the coast he had workers' houses constructed that he offered to the tenant farmers who unwillingly left their thatched cottages isolated in the Highland valleys. In reality he contributed to the depopulation of the Highlands. Over 5000 families were evicted from the homes of their ancestors. Their place was taken by the sheep that are still today a constant feature of the region's landscape. During the last century almost the whole of the county of Sutherland in the Northwestern Highlands, that is to say, 1,300,000 acres of land, were owned by the Duchy, making it one of the greatest landowners of Western Europe. The current French-style castle owes its appearance to the 2nd Duke who in circa 1850 summoned Charles Barry, the architect of the House of Parliament in Westminster, in order to transform Dunrobin from a Scottish castle into a stately home. His wife, the Duchess Harriet, was a lady-in-waiting to Queen Victoria. The 3rd Duke constructed at his own expense the Highlands railway and the Victorian-style station that can still be seen not far from the castle. The castle itself features a library with a gigantic globe and hunting trophies and a Sicilian-style bedroom suite acquired by the Duke during a cruise through the Mediterranean. The castle is surrounded by a large park and an Italian garden with borders of roses and shrubs.

90-91 and 91
The new design for the drawing room, which was rebuilt after the fire of 1915, combined two smaller rooms so as to create a large airy salon with a beautiful view over the garden surrounding the great fountain. The ceilings, designed by Robert Lorimer, were created by Sam Wheeler in 1919. The furniture is from the Louis XV period, while the walls are covered with 18th-century tapestries depicting the life of the Greek philosopher Diogenes. The finest works are, however, the masterpieces by Canaletto hanging over the fireplaces.

91 top left The original billiards room designed by Lorimer is today used for the exposition of family heirlooms and ceremonial costumes. The billiards table has been placed in the Gallery, where hunting trophies can be seen behind the arches.

92 top A portrait painted by James Currie of William, 22nd Brodie of Brodie, together with his family, his wife Elizabeth Ballie of Redcastle and three of the couple's four children.

92 bottom The vaulted ceiling richly decorated with stucco-work is the main feature of this room. The writing desk with its scalloped edge dates from the Louis XV period, as does the rounded chest.

S et in a 70-hectare park a few miles to the east of Nairn, for over eight centuries Brodie Castle was the home of the Brodie family. The castle dates from the fifteenth century with additions and extensions from the sixteenth, but it is thought that the original nucleus was first inhabited by the Brodies in 1160. All of the documentation relating to the origins of the castle and its rebuilding around 1560 was lost in the fire of 1645 when Lord Lewis Gordon, representing the Duke of Montrose, torched the castle during the civil war against the Covenanters. The castle was rebuilt and took on its present appearance in the seventeenth and eighteenth centuries. It features a Z-shaped plan with overhanging turrets and battlements. The extensions to the east, north and northeast made in 1824 are in the neo-Tudor style and were designed by William Burn. The oldest part of the building is the semi-basement kitchen in the North Wing. In 1982 ownership of the castle passed to the National Trust for Scotland.

92-93 Famous for the flowering of many varieties of daffodils in early spring, Brodie Castle is a tower house built on a Z-shaped plan that has developed over the centuries. It is surrounded by a park with nature trails that reach the marsh where wild birds can be observed.

93 top left At the center of the dining room, a large table is surrounded by sixteen chairs dating from around 1840. The table is laid with porcelain plates bearing the coat of arms and motto of the family. Hanging on the walls are portraits recounting centuries of family history.

93 top right The family coat of arms is composed of a shield and the motto "unite" and is seen here in one of the castle's windows. Historians believe the Brodie family descends from a Celtic tribe rewarded with land by Malcom III. The original surname was Brothie and was modified to Brodie early in the 16th century.

*J*ust a few miles from Inverness and the Moray Firth, the Castle of Cawdor is associated with the Shakespearean tragedy, *Macbeth*. The tower with its entrance raised as a defensive measure, was built in 1380 by William Thane of Cawdor, a friend of King James II. Legend has it that a dream prompted him to allow a mule loaded with gold to roam freely and to build a castle at the very place where the animal stopped to sleep. The mule lay down beneath a hawthorn tree around which the original tower was constructed, arranged on four storys linked by a spiral staircase. In 1638 work began on the north wing and the old sitting room was linked by a stone staircase.

94 top left and 94-95 The gardens surrounding Cawdor Castle have a very intimate atmosphere. They are at their best from spring to late summer. The recently restored walled garden offers attractive combinations of colors.

94 bottom left and 95 top The severe, massive Cawdor Castle was built on a slight rise as the private fortress of the Thanes of Cawdor. In spite of the additions made over the centuries, it still has the appearance of a tower house with corner turrets and battlements.

94 right The family coat of arms is set into the walls of the castle that William Shakespeare used as the setting for the tragedy Macbeth *with the assassination of Duncan.*

96 top In spite of its bleak external appearance, Cawdor Castle has a surprisingly comfortable internal atmosphere. This is not so surprising when you consider that the castle is still the family home. Not all of the rooms are open to the public; the private areas include the intimate and welcoming dining and drawing rooms seen here.

96-97 The drawing room occupies what was once the old hall. The last major rebuilding work dates from the 16th century when a fireplace with the coat of arms of the Calders, the old form of Cawdor was added. Portraits of members of the family such as Pryse Campbell, the 18th Thane of Cawdor, dressed in an assortment of tartans, hang on the walls.

During the civil war the castle escaped lightly with only a few haylofts being torched by the royalist troops led by Lord Montrose. During Cromwell's bloody campaigns Cawdor Castle was allowed not to have to house soldiers and officers, thus safeguarding its rich interior furnishings. In 1684 the castle was transformed into a comfortable home by Sir Hugh Campbell, the 15th Thane. The windows were enlarged, carved fireplaces were installed and two new wings to house the Thane's nine children and numerous servants were built. Further improvements were made around 1720 and the middle of the nineteenth century, but without leading to significant modifications.

97 top The dining room features a late-Victorian style decorated ceiling and tapestries with scenes from the life of Don Quixote on the walls.

97 bottom The stairs are covered with a carpet that features the colors of the Campbell of Cawdor tartan. Antique firearms are arranged on the walls.

98 top left The upper valley of the River Dee is one of the most beautiful and gentlest areas of the Scottish Highlands. The salmon-rich river flows between fertile pastures at the foot of bare hills.

98 top right The attractive drawing room has an informal atmosphere. It features pink walls and 19th-century Persian carpets on the floor. Among the paintings is a portrait of Mrs. Farquharson of Invercauld, the grandmother of the current Lord.

98-99 In contrast with the lavish decoration of other castles in their area, Braemar Castle appears stark, with few windows and no ornamental features. Only the movement of the turrets and battlements enlivens the architecture. The interiors are also simple, almost austere, and testify to the style of life in a Highlands castle.

99 top Adjacent to the dining room, the Morning Room is simple and free of fripperies. Hanging on the walls are portraits of John, the Earl of Mar who built the castle, and one of his descendant, also called John, who led the revolt of 1715.

99 bottom On the first floor of the castle, the dining room has a simple fireplace and a large central table. Note the two globes, one terrestrial and the other depicting the heavens, dating from 1818. A piece of the plaid worn by the Young Pretender, Bonnie Prince Charlie, together with other relics testifying to the family's Jacobite sympathies, are exhibited in this room.

BRAEMAR CASTLE

*B*raemar is a small village in the upper valley of the River Dee, famous throughout the world for the Royal Highlands Gathering, the traditional Highland games held each summer in the presence of the royal family.

Standing against the magnificent backdrop of the peaks of the Cairngorms the castle has a severe aspect, animated only by the play of turrets and battlements. It was built in 1628 by John Erskine, the Earl of Mar and the treasurer to King James VI. The fortress served as a lodge during hunting trips organized in the Grampian mountains, but also as a bulwark against the increasing power of the Farquharsons. In 1689, during the brief Jacobite rebellion, the castle was conquered and burned by the "Black Colonel," John Farquharson of Inverary, and for sixty years remained a ruined shell. The 39th Earl of Mar inspired the Jacobite rebellion of 1715, on the 6th of September of that year brought together the rebel troops at Braemar, where today stands the Invercauld Arms Hotel. At that time the castle was but a blackened skeleton and was requisitioned by the loyalist troops following the defeat of Mar and the Jacobites at Sheriffmuir. The castle was restored in 1748 and transformed into a garrison for the troops of the Hanoverian government. The very young Adam brothers, John and Robert, had a hand in

the reconstruction and went on, of course, to become extremely famous architects. The crenellated curtain wall dates from this period and was based on a star-shaped plan in accordance with Renaissance theories on fortifications.

At the end of the century the castle was converted back into a residence and housed Queen Victoria when she came to attend the Highland Games prior to the acquisition of Balmoral.

BLAIR CASTLE

et in the heart of the wild Grampian mountains, Blair Castle has always controlled the main road between Edinburgh and Inverness. Its history is closely linked to that of Scotland itself and the struggles between the Highland clans.

The residence of the Dukes of Atholl ever since the time of the Celts, the castle was actually built in 1269 by John Cumming of Badenoch who

took advantage of the absence of the Earl, David, who was involved in the crusades. Hidden amidst the turrets and battlements there is the original tower, still known today as the Cumming Tower.

Over the centuries the castle was subjected to diverse modifications and additions. It also changed hands on a number of occasions due to a lack of heirs or political maneuvering. In 1457 the deeds to the estate were given by James I to his blood brother Sir John Stewart of Balvenie, the founder of the current dynasty and whose motto, conferred by King James III together with the order to put down the insurrection of the MacDonalds in the islands, was "Furth Fortune and fill the Fetters."

The male line was extinguished in 1625 and the title to the castle passed to John Murray, Lord of Tullibardine and a descendant on the maternal side. After his death, Blair Castle was occupied by the Duke of Montrose and in 1652 by Cromwell's troops. Claverhouse, the leader of the Jacobite rebellion, occupied the castle in 1689 and on the 27th of July of that year recorded a famous victory over the government troops in the narrow gorge of the River Garry near Killiecrankie.

The extension and rebuilding of the castle undertaken by the 2nd Duke was interrupted by the Jacobite revolt of 1745 when the pretender to the throne, Bonnie Prince Charlie, marched south with his army of Highlanders, staying for some days at Blair Castle.

100 top The tapestry room on the second floor of Cumming Tower owes its name to the sumptuous tapestries woven in Brussels for Charles I.

100 bottom On the staircase, below a richly stuccoed ceiling, hang portraits of members of the family: the 1st Duke, John, immortalized by Thomas Murray, the 1st Marquis of Atholl, John, depicted by Jacob De Witt in the guise of Julius Caesar, and his wife, Lady Amelia Stanley.

100-101 When Queen Victoria visited Blair Castle in 1844 she described it as a "broad and simple white building." Twenty-five years later the 7th Duke commissioned John and David Bryce to rebuild the castle in the Scottish Baronial style we see today.

101 top The white structure of Blair Castle with its crenellated towers and conical roofs stands out against the green mountains of the central Highlands. Around the castle extends a large estate with sheep pastures, woods, gardens and cultivated land.

102 top The drawing room is the most beautiful room in Blair Castle, with walls covered with crimson damask silk and a ceiling decorated with elaborate stucco-work. Above the white marble fireplace hangs a family portrait by Johann Zoffany depicting the 3rd Duke, his wife and their seven children.

102-103 The Ballroom was built between 1876 and 1877 by the 7th Duke. Beneath a wooden ceiling with exposed beams, this room was used for balls, concerts, receptions and the world bagpipe championships. The partially paneled walls are decorated with various family portraits and hunting trophies.

103 top
The Tea Room boasts a rich collection of dinner and tea services. One of the rarest is the 18th-century oriental service with the coat of arms of the Dukes of Atholl.

103 bottom
The wood-paneled entrance hall was built by the 7th Duke. In pride of place at the center is the portrait of Iain, the last Duke, executed by the painter Carlos Sancha in 1982, on

the occasion of the 25th anniversary of the Duke's accession to the title. A rich collection of arms (guns, pistols, swords, bows and crossbows) are arranged in decorative patterns on the walls.

After being occupied by the troops of the reigning Hanoverian dynasty, in 1746 the castle was besieged by Lord George Murray, the 2nd Duke, at the head of his Atholl Highlanders. This was the last castle in Great Britain ever to be besieged and ironically enough it was by the owner himself. Once the situation had been resolved the 2nd Duke revived his modernization work, following the dominant Georgian style. In 1756 the portrait staircase on the walls of which the Lords of Atholl are immortalized was added. The last intervention dates from the late nineteenth century when between 1869 and 1904, the castle was restored in a Romantic vein. Today it is a white turreted manor house surrounded by an immense forest and pastures with hundreds of sheep.

The last Duke of Atholl, the 10th, who died in 1996 was also the only man in the entire United Kingdom with the right to maintain a private army, the Atholl Highlanders. On his death, the castle and the 70,000-acre estate was inherited by a charitable institute. The title on the other hand went to a distant South African cousin.

BALMORAL CASTLE

104 top left A vast estate extends around Balmoral and ranges from the fertile lands of the valley to the heather-covered hills of the Lochnagar range dominating the area.

104 bottom left The tower stands out from the western façade, rising from the main body of the building, and at the top, below the arrow slits, can be seen a large clock.

Balmoral Castle, the summer residence of the royal family, stands in the upper Dee valley, not far from Braemar. Set at the foot of wooded hills, the castle is surrounded by a vast estate acquired in 1848 by Prince Albert and Queen Victoria, who had both fallen in love with the Highlands. When the royal couple visited Balmoral for the first time Queen Victoria described it in her diary as "a pretty little castle in the Scottish style, surrounded by wooded hills that recall Turingia, the birthplace of Prince Albert." The castle was actually two hundred years old but had been rebuilt a few years earlier by the previous owner, Sir Robert Gordon. The building was not large enough for the needs of the royal family, for their numerous servants and for their state obligations.

In 1852 work thus began on the construction of a new castle in the Gothic Revival style to the designs of the architect William Smith. The new residence in white granite was completed over the following years, while the royal family spent the summers in the old castle. Balmoral is composed of a massive square tower, embellished with four lateral towers and a long three-story wing with large panoramic windows that led Queen Victoria to write, "Not only is the house attractive and comfortable but it has a beautiful view, that the old castle did not."

*104 top right
The west wing of the palace overlooks the magnificent and painstakingly groomed Rose Garden with the statue of a chamois and the fountain. The luxuriant gardens are at their best when the royal family is in residence at Balmoral during the summer.*

*104 bottom right
A family portrait with Queen Victoria at Windsor Castle in 1890 and views of the Balmoral and Sandringham. The images were reproduced in the volume published on the occasion of the sovereign's jubilee.*

105 This aerial view reveals the layout of Balmoral Castle as a whole. The present-day structure is the fruit of numerous modifications made over the years to adapt the summer residence to the needs of the royal family.

*106 The Ballroom,
the walls of which
feature a bas-relief
by John Thomas,
overlooks the granite
steps built in 1857
that lead to the fertile
banks of the River
Dee.*

*107 The Ballroom is
the only room of the
castle open to the
public. Family
portraits and objects
of royal provenance
are exhibited in the
great room
illuminated by tall
windows.*

108 top Dunvegan Castle is the only stately home in the Western Isles and is the house inhabited the longest by a single family in the whole of Scotland. Among the visitors to the castle were James V and Sir Walter Scott.

108-109 and 109 top All around Dunvegan Castle extends a large park crossed by footpaths that lead to two spectacular waterfalls. The benign influence of the Gulf Stream allows plants typical of lower latitudes such as rhododendrons and azaleas to flourish. A short distance away, on the sea shore, colonies of seals bask in the warmth of the sun.

DUNVEGAN CASTLE

*O*verlooking Loch Dunvegan on the northwest side of the Isle of Skye, this castle has always been the home of the MacLeods, the lords of the isles. Tradition has it that Leod was the youngest son of the last Viking king of the Isle of Man and the Hebrides. When King Alexander II defeated the Vikings in 1263 at Lairg, Leod possessed at least half of the Hebrides.

The land of the MacLeods is still extensive but is today restricted to part of the Isle of Skye, Dunvegan Castle and its surroundings up to the Cuillins which rise barren and steep 3260 feet above sea level.

In the thirteenth century, during the period of the first clan chieftain, the castle was no more than a defensive wall protecting a low building with a thatched roof. Around 1340, Malcom, the third MacLeod chieftain, added a massive square tower at the northeast corner of the house.

At the southeast corner there is an elegant fairy-tale tower built at the behest of Alasdair, the 8th chieftain, in around 1500. The tower's four floors are linked by a spiral staircase.

The present Romantic appearance dates from the Victorian era when the castle was extended between 1840 and 1850 by the 25th clan chieftain, to the designs of the architect Robert Brown of Edinburgh. The work cost the notable sum of 11,250 $.

109 bottom
For seven centuries the castle has belonged to the MacLeods and is associated with the legend of The Fairy Flag, a mysterious and extremely old silk banner of Middle Eastern origin which is said to have the magical ability to rescue the clan from peril. It is said to have been presented to a member of the MacLeod clan by an enamored fairy.

*110 top
The spectacular ruins of the Marischals' impregnable fortress, Dunnottar Castle, stand on a cliff falling sheer to the North Sea near Aberdeen. The castle put up stubborn resistance to Cromwell's besieging troops.*

CENTRAL AND EASTERN SCOTLAND

Undulating countryside that gives way to wooded hills, bucolic valleys that gradually transform in heather-covered moors: that central and eastern Scotland is a rich and fertile region is demonstrated by the dozens of castles constructed along the course of the River Dee or on Tayside, with a concentration greater than in any other part of the country, with the possible exception of the area around Edinburgh. This is the region of the royal castles of Stirling and Falkland and those of the manors tied to the crown such as Drummond and Glamis. But above all, it is the area in which the Scottish Baronial style of architecture with its towers, battlements and overhangs on a generally simple and linear base can be seen to best effect in buildings such as Craigievar Castle, Castle Fraser and Fyvie Castle.

Numerous stone circles show that these hospitable lands have been inhabited since prehistoric times. The earliest settlers were the Picts who lived here long before the Celts reached Scotland. The Roman legions arrived between the 1st and the 2nd centuries, established their base near Mons Grapius close to the present-day Stonehaven and there defeated the Scottish tribes. They did not remain for long, however, preferring to withdraw south of the wall constructed by Antoninus between the Clyde and the Firth of Forth.

In the 9th century Kenneth MacAlpine united the kingdom of Dalriada with that of the Picts, thus gaining control of much of Scotland. The capital of the new kingdom stood not far from Scone Palace, built with the stones of the ancient abbey. The thirteenth century saw power pass into the hands of the Comyns, the Counts of Buchan, following the marriage between a Comyn and the daughter of a local chieftain. Robert the Bruce's fight against the English was also a struggle against the Comyns, their allies. Then came the turn of the Gordons who exercised almost regal control over the northeast until 1562. This was the century in which the simple Medieval tower houses began to be transformed into vertical palaces. A typical example is Crathes Castle in the Dee valley, built towards the end of the sixteenth century. From the same period, and at a short distance away, is Castle Fraser which features decorative elements of French origin. Haddo House, designed by William Adam for one of the branches of the powerful Gordon family, was built in the Neoclassical and Georgian styles.

110-111 Over 400 years of history are enclosed within the powerful walls of Castle Fraser. Built in 1575 near Aberdeen by Michael Fraser, the 6th Lord, the two low wings help to emphasize the attractive central tower, making it one of the most beautiful castles in Scotland.

111 Built in sandstone, Kellie Castle in Fife dates from the 14th century. In 1573 a second tower was added to the east and the castle was completed between 1573 and 1605. The southeast tower, with the entrance portal, is a minor masterpiece with overhangs and corner turrets. The gardens are extremely attractive.

FYVIE CASTLE

112 top left and 113 top Fyvie Castle is surrounded by a great English-style park with ponds and lakes. The walled garden which features informal combinations of flowers of all colors is of immense appeal. The park is embellished with sculptures such as the statue of the dwarf of Queen Henrietta Maria, or the 16th-century urn sculpted from Venetian marble.

Fyvie is a village set amidst the woods on the banks of the River Ythan, once famous for its freshwater pearls. Surrounded by a great park with a small lake, the castle is one of the best examples of Scottish Baronial architecture, with five towers commemorating the five great families to have owned the estate through the ages, the Prestons, the Meldrums, the Setons, the Gordons and the Forbes-Leiths.

Originally Fyvie was a royal fortress, surrounded by a hunting forest, as indicated by the Gaelic place name which means Hill of Deer. The castle occupied a strategic position: to the east it was protected by a great marsh and to the north and the west by the meanders of the river. The only line of attack was from the south where the single, well defended entrance led into an internal courtyard.

The oldest castle on the site was probably built in wood, with external defences in beaten earth. William the Lion visited Fyvie in 1211 (or 1214) and Alexander III conceded its statute to him. On the 31st of July, 1296, the English King Edward occupied Fyvie during his punitive campaign in Scotland. Some years later Robert the Bruce administered justice in the an open-air court in the castle's beech forests.

In the fourteenth century the castle took the form of a massive stone keep protected by a high curtain wall reinforced with corner turrets.

112 bottom left and 112-113 A jewel of Scottish architecture, Fyvie Castle emerges from the green countryside with towers and spires that are decoratively topped with statues of musicians. The castle is the fruit of repeated and successive modifications that fortunately have not compromised its harmonious architecture.

112 top right The coat of arms of the Forbes-Leith family, the last owners of the castle. In 1889, Alexander Leith, an American steel magnate, acquired the castle and embellished it with works of art.

The principal entrance through the south wall was defended by further towers, in all likelihood constructed during the period of Edward I's occupation.

The castle remained the property of the Crown until 1370 when it was presented by Robert II to his eldest son John, the future Robert III who in his turn presented it to his cousin, Sir James Lindsay, Lord of Crawford and Buchan. In 1390-91 Fyvie was reassigned to Sir Henry Preston, a cousin of Sir James, who took possession only in 1402. Having become the property of the Medurn family through marriage, Fyvie was sold in 1596 to Alexander Seton, the Chancellor of Scotland, who undertook major extension works and the creation of the triumphant ornamentation of the top floor and the roof that made of this castle a fairy-tale composition of overhanging turrets, decorated pediments, sculpted garrets and pinnacles in the form of hunters or musicians.

Support for the Jacobite cause led to the requisitioning of the Fyvie estate and, in 1694, Seton's grandson died penniless in a Parisian attic where he had fled after having backed the unsuccessful revolution of the Stuarts.

In 1733 Fyvie Castle was acquired by the 2nd Duke of Aberdeen for his third marriage and it was subsequently inherited by the first-born son of this union, William Gordon of Fyvie.

CHARTA ROBERTI III IN FAVOREM HENRICI DE PRESTOUNE MILITIS

PRO REDEMPTIONE RADULPHI DE PERCY MILITIS ANGLICI ET PROSERVITIO SUO OMNIUM TERRARUM BARONIO DE FERMARTYN INFRA VICECOMITATUM DE ABIRDENE

114-115 The entrance hall, furnished by William Gordon, replaced the old fortified entrance on the south side of the castle. The ceilings are richly decorated and the walls are covered with hunting trophies, arms and armor collected by Lord Leith. The armor came from Germany and dates back to the 16th-17th

century. One can also admire a marble bust of Caesar Augustus and the perfectly preserved tusk of an elephant. The most impressive element of the furnishings is the fireplace, surmounted by a relief panel illustrating the Battle of Otterburn of 1388 in which Sir Henry Preston captured Ralph de Percy.

115 top left The dining room was furnished by William Gordon in 1790 and subsequently modified by Lord Leith. The red wall covering, the dark draperies and the stucco-work on the ceiling confer an austere and ceremonial atmosphere upon the room. There are numerous portraits hanging on the wall:

above the fireplace, in a carved wood frame, is the wife of Lord Leith, Marie Louise January; on the door to the servant's quarters hangs a portrait of Lord Leith himself while portraits of Sir William Maxwell of Calderwood and Sir John Stirling of Kippendarie with his daughter hang on the other walls.

115 bottom left A portrait of Ethel Louise Forbes-Leith painted by Luke Fildes in 1906 dominates the Back Morning Room. The sole heir of Alexander Leith, on the death of her father in 1925 she inherited the title that was eventually passed on to her son Andrew, born in 1929.

115 top right and bottom The Billiards Room is located at the base of the Gordon Tower, in what were until 1890 the kitchens. This room was the favorite of the male members of the family for games, smoking and drinking. The billiards table was made by Cox and Yeman of London. Various paintings with Scottish subjects hang on the walls: the most spectacular is The Sound of Many Waters painted by Sir John Millais. Another depicts the Scots Greys at Waterloo, painted by Colonel F.S. Seccombe in 1891. Hunting trophies and arms are displayed above the fireplace. The castle also boasts an unusual room for bowling.

At the end of the eighteenth century the new owner drained the marsh on the east side, created a lake, landscaped the park and added the Gordon Tower to the north of the West Wing. In 1885 his descendant, Sir Maurice Duff Gordon was obliged to sell the family estate to resolve his financial difficulties.

Four years later Fyvie Castle and its lands were acquired for 246,130 $

by Alexander Leith, a Scotsman born at Blackford, a few miles from the castle, who had made a fortune in America, becoming one of the magnates of the steel industry. During his lifetime he embellished the castle with suits of armor, tapestries and paintings of the English and Scottish Schools. In 1890 he added the Leith Tower to the west of the Gordon Tower. In 1983, Sir Andrew Forbes-Leith put the property up for sale and after long negotiations it was sold to the National Trust for Scotland.

116 top left The portrait of William Gordon of Fyvie by the Italian Pompeo Batoni is one of the most interesting works of the 18th century. Painted in 1766, it differs from other portraits by the artist who generally lent a gentle air to his aristocratic sitters. Sir William instead wanted to be portrayed as a proud Scotsman in the family tartan, standing in front of the Coliseum as a reference to the heroes of the Roman empire. This portrait is one of the most valuable works preserved at Fyvie Castle.

116 top right and 116-117 The atmosphere of the Music Room which leads off the drawing rooms is typical of the Edwardian style of many British homes of the early 20th century; a blend of antique and modern. The walls are covered with 17th-century tapestries from Brussels woven to the original designs of Peter Paul Rubens. The French Renaissance is well represented by the marble fireplace dating from 1521 featuring extremely colorful tiles with oriental motifs that can clearly be seen in the detail. The organ and the tiffany lamp complete the precious furnishings of this room.

117 top This drawing room on the second floor of the Gordon Tower was built in 1790 as the Morning Room by General William Gordon and was subsequently modified. On the ceiling the stucco-work represents the family coat of arms. With its dark red draperies, the room reflects the tastes of the 18th century. The imposing portrait of General William Gordon painted by Pompeo Batoni is from this era. Above the mantlepiece hangs a portrait of Susanna Archer, the Countess of Oxford, by Sir Thomas Lawrence. Other valuable paintings bear the signatures of Gainsborough, Reynolds and Romney. The furnishing is prevalently Victorian or Edwardian, while the cabinets are in the Louis XV style.

117 bottom The small library contains a rich collection of books dealing with Scottish history and literature and topographical maps. This room was used by Lord Leith as a study. On his desk two electric bells kept him in contact with his assistants. Nautical decoration on the ceiling recalls Lord Leith's own naval career and his father's past as an admiral. Above the door hangs a copy of the portrait of William Elphinstone.

118 top left
This portrait of Lord
Haddo was painted
by Pompeo Batoni,
an Italian exponent
of the early neo-
classical style.

118 top right
Haddo House was
designed in 1731
by William Adam
for the 2nd Earl of
Aberdeen. Many of
the splendid interiors
date from the end of
19th century.

HADDO HOUSE

118-119 The library occupies the old stable block and is paneled in cedar wood inlaid with ebony. The rare books reflect the 4th Earl's interest in Greek and Latin texts and travel writing. All of the furnishings and the decor date back to the 19th century.

119 left The Morning Room occupies what in Adam's original design were three bedrooms. Transformed into a library by the 4th Earl, the space was eventually transformed into an informal sitting room. The fireplace, the mirror and the stucco-work date from the end of the 19th century. Note, between the two windows, the Irish satinwood cabinet given to the 7th Earl by his wife to commemorate his mandate in Ireland.

When Haddo house was built in the eighteenth century by William Gordon, the 2nd Earl of Aberdeen, to the designs of William Adam, the most famous Scottish architect of the day, it astonished the local nobility accustomed to living in romantic but hardly comfortable turreted castles. The great Palladian house with its two circular corridors linking the lateral wings contrasted with the barren surroundings of eastern Scotland. The construction of Haddo House was extremely expensive, partly because the finest materials were used. These included Norwegian timber for the roof which was completed in 1734 while the second wing was finished a year later. The ambitious Earl was not short of money, however, and he was known as a hard, inflexible land owner who exploited his tenants to the full. The 2nd Earl of Aberdeen died in 1745 and left the house to his son George, the 3rd Earl, a son from his first marriage (the heirs from the 3rd marriage instead received Fyvie Castle), but his amorous relations and worldly lifestyle left him with little time to devote to

property. It was George's grandson George Gordon, the 4th Earl, orphaned at 12 years of age and educated at Cambridge, who took Haddo House in hand. His interest in the Italian Renaissance led him to Italy, Greece, Turkey, Albania, Austria and Germany and resulted in him becoming known as the Athenian of Aberdeen. George Gordon took up a political career and between 1828 and 1830 was the Secretary of State for Foreign Affairs and between 1834 and 1835 the Secretary of State for the colonies. In 1852 he was entrusted by Queen Victoria with the task of forming a new government. Early in this century the 4th Earl commissioned the architect Archibald Simpson to extend Haddo House. William Adam's circular corridors were demolished and the lateral wings were extended: the North Wing contained the stables while the South Wing was reserved for the kitchens and the servants' quarters. Gordon summoned James Giles, a painter and garden designer, for the landscaping of the grounds. The last extension of Haddo House was made at the behest of the 7th Earl who, in 1877, revised the lateral elements in order to create new chambers for the family. In 1880 the architects Wardrop and Reid of Edinburgh definitively transformed the house to make it more suitable to the changing demands of the family. The new arrangement of the entrance and the staircase robbed the western façade of the purity of William Adam's neo-classical design.

119 top right The dining room has been preserved with its 1880 furnishings intact. Portraits of the family and of the Stuarts hang on the walls. The attractive table is laid with silver, crystal and porcelain.

119 bottom right Redecorated at the end of the 19th century, the drawing room at Haddo House is dominated by the painting of David and Goliath by Domenichino that hangs above the fireplace. Among the other pictures exhibited are a Head of St. Peter by Van Dyck and a portrait of Sir Walter Scott and his daughter by Sir William Allan.

CRAIGIEVAR CASTLE

120 left Craigievar Castle, a forebear of far more modern constructions, develops vertically. To climb the spiral staircase that links each floor is to take a leap into history and to experience first hand the lifestyle of an aristocratic Scottish family of the early 17th century.

120 top right The Queen's Room is dominated by a magnificent four-poster bed. The walls are covered with wood panels by Scottish craftsmen while above the fireplace one can admire two portraits depicting the 5th Baronet and his wife painted in 1788 by Raeburn for the modest sum of 16 guineas.

Set in a secluded position in the picturesque Grampian Hills, Craigievar Castle is universally recognized as the best example of a tower house built in Scotland, a happy marriage of local tradition and exotic influences of French origin. Three storys rise on an L-shaped plan, with four in the central tower. In reality the castle is a house built vertically rather than horizontally, with spiral staircases taking the place of corridors. While the lower section is simple and austere, the upper floors are a play of projections, turrets, parapets and spires.

The first reference to Craigievar is found in a statute of 1457 conserved in the castle itself, which indicates the owners of the castle as the Mortimer family. The Mortimers began the construction of the castle, but late in the sixteenth century they suffered financial problems and were obliged to stop work and sell the property. The new lord of Craigievar Castle was William Forbes, the brother of the Archbishop of Aberdeen and a merchant who had made a fortune trading with the Baltic ports, earning himself the nickname Danzig Willie. The profits from his commercial enterprises refinanced the construction of the castle, leaving great expressive freedom to the master mason. Since then the descendants of the merchant have lived for centuries in the castle. In 1963 the property was donated to the National Trust for Scotland, a body that manages dozens of places of historical interest.

120 bottom right Little has changed since the Hall was completed in 1626. The vaulted ceiling was covered with decorated stucco-work and medallions with portraits. Wood oak panels with neo-classical details are on the walls and the carpet shows the green and blue Forbes tartan.

121 Craigievar Castle stands isolated and austere in the gentle hills to the north of the River Dee. This splendid example of Scottish architecture is an elegant blend of elements drawn from the local tradition and foreign influences.

122 top left The Long Gallery takes up the whole length of one wing of the castle and is famous for its vaulted ceiling decorated with oak panels, one of the few in Scotland, with the exception of those of the royal palaces. In this century it was transformed into a library.

122 top right The name "Muse's Room" derives from the decoration of the ceiling depicting the Nine Muses and Seven Virtues. The female figures have led to a suggestion that the room was originally a ladies' drawing room. There is a particularly attractive tapestry designed by William Morris.

122-123 and 123 right The gardens at Crathes Castle are divided into eight thematic zones, set on two different levels and separated by yew hedges. They have been designed so that plants are flowering all year round. The layout can be clearly seen in this aerial photograph.

123 left A gardener intent on transforming a yew shrub into a sculpture. The gardens are tended by four gardeners supervised by a head gardener. Much of the current layout was designed by Sir James Burnett and his wife, Lady Sybil, both green-thumbed enthusiasts.

Along with Craigievar, Crathes Castle is one of the best examples of Scottish architecture. Begun in 1553 by Alexander Burnett, it took over forty years to complete the fortress with its L-shaped plan, and it was finished thanks to his great-grandson. In 1656 it was inhabited by Burnett's grandson, the 12th Lord. The history of the building is commemorated in two shields on the eastern façade. The first contains the coat of arms of Alexander Burnett and Janet Hamilton with the date on which work began, the second contains those of Alexander Burnett (the great-grandson) and Katherine Gordon and the date it was completed.

Like all the castles in the Scottish baronial style, Crathes develops vertically. The upper part is a triumph of turrets, overhangs, pinnacles and false battlements while the lower section is more austere, in spite of the opening of Victorian-style windows on the first floor. During the last century an incongruous late-Victorian wing overlooking the upper garden was added. Destroyed in a fire in 1966, it is today restored, but the Victorian additions were not rebuilt. The magnificent eighteenth century grounds feature one of the richest collections of trees in the whole of Great Britain.

GLAMIS CASTLE

G lamis Castle, the home of the 18th Earl of Strathmore and Kinghorne, is one of the most famous castles in Scotland and the birthplace of Princess Margaret. A grandiose avenue leads to a fortified manor house in pink sandstone, all turrets and pinnacles, the result of the romantic additions of the nineteenth century.

Originally the castle was one of the many hunting lodges of the kings of Scotland, although the site had already been inhabited in earlier times. Around the eighth century St. Fergus had built a church there of which a sacred wall remains.

In 1372 Sir John Lyon received the Glamis estate as a gift from King Robert II and four years later he married the King's daughter Joanna. The castle of the epoch is incorporated in the present building, the ramified structure of which is the result of successive extensions. Originally the castle took the form of a tall, slim tower that was easily defended but provided inconvenient living accommodation. The ground floor was occupied by storerooms while the principal hall was located on the first floor and was reached via an external staircase.

In spite of the Lyon family's ties of kinship and centuries of fidelity to the Crown, in the sixteenth century it was deprived of royal support. The cause of the family's disgrace was the marriage between John, sixteenth Lord of Glamis, and a Douglas, the sister of the Earl of Angus, who was suspected of treason.

124 top and 125 top right On the lawn in front of the entrance to the castle stands a baroque sundial with diverse faces, decorated with rampant lions. Together with the turrets and the statues of James VI and his son Charles I, they are all that remain of the walls that once surrounded the castle.

124 bottom The detail shot of a roof shows the sculptural decoration at the summit of Glamis.

124-125 This aerial view of the castle highlights the intricate design of the upper section, a feature of all the Scottish Baronial castles: the conical roofs of the towers and turrets, the battlements and the chimneys.

125 top left This plaque on the façade depicts the coat of arms of the Earl of Strathmore and Kinghorne: a lion and a horse rampant support a shield surmounted by a cross and closed with the motto "In te domine speravi."

126 top left The whole wing housing the dining room was demolished and rebuilt between 1775 and 1801. In 1851-53 the son of the 8th Duke of Strathmore designed this room with its unusual ceiling, an impressive fireplace and oak paneling bearing the coat of arms of the 12th Duke of Strathmore.

126 bottom left This room occupies, in all probability, the former bedroom of the primitive hunting lodge. Its name, King Malcom's Room, is purely commemorative. The stucco-work decorating the ceiling is particularly fine.

126 bottom right The Queen Mother's Sitting Room is part of the royal apartments created by the Countess of Strathmore following the marriage of her daughter to the future George VI in 1923. The atmosphere is welcoming with tapestries, carpets and pink curtains. The dark, carved oak fireplace contrasts with the precious Chinese and Dutch porcelain exhibited on its shelves.

127 The pale pink color scheme of the drawing room enhances the gilded frames of the portraits on the walls. The ceiling is decorated with fine stucco-work featuring heraldic motifs. Among the paintings, the one by Auchterhouse portraying the 3rd Duke of Strathmore with his sons John, Charles and Patrick Lyon is worthy of particular mention.

126 top right The lion rampant in brass in the dining room is one of the symbols of the Bowes-Lyon family. It was a present on the occasion of the 13th Earl's golden wedding anniversary in 1903.

126 center right The billiards room, built between 1773 and 1776, has a relaxing atmosphere, the walls being lined with

antique books and precious tapestries made in the 17th century. The stucco-work on the ceiling dates from 1903 and commemorates the 13th Earl's golden wedding anniversary. The large fireplace decorated with coats of arms came from Gibside, a property belonging to the Bowes family in the county of Durham.

Following the death of her husband, Lady Glamis was accused of witchcraft, imprisoned until she became blind and then burned alive in the square in front of Edinburgh Castle. Her young son was also imprisoned and the family property was requisitioned by the Crown. Thus between 1537 and 1542, James V, the future father of Mary Stuart, held court at Glamis with many royal edicts emanating from the castle. On the sovereign's death, John, the 7th Lord of Glamis, was liberated and, thanks to an Act of Parliament, regained his property. The furniture and silver had, however, disappeared following the passage to the royal court. John, the 8th Lord and the Chancellor of Scotland, restored the castle to its former glories. According to one of his guests, an English ambassador, the staff consisted of a butler, two manservants, a musician, a chief cook, a cellar master, a master mason, a head porter with his assistants, a bailiff and an officer. The lady of the house was attended by two ladies in waiting, a seamstress, a personal chambermaid and two further servants.

John's son Patrick was made Earl of Kinghorne by James VI whom he followed to London when, on the death of Elizabeth, the king of Scotland also became James I King of England. Patrick began to make a series of improvements to the castle which resulted in its present appearance, but misfortune was once again to strike at the doors of Glamis.

128 left Although
the castle has been
subjected to diverse
modifications over
the centuries, the
stairs leading to the
crypt and the dining
room still have a
Medieval air.
A lateral staircase
leads to the Hall.

128 right The King's
Room is part of the
royal apartments.
Originally it was the
dressing room of King
George VI. The room
is dominated by a
large four-poster bed
made for the 1st Earl
of Kinghorne early
in the 17th century.

John ran up huge debts in his support of the cause of the Covenanters
who fought against the Church and
the episcopacy. His successor Patrick,
the 3rd Earl, thus found himself sad-
dled with the astronomical debt of
$56,260. In 1670 he arrived at
Glamis with his wife and began
working to redress the situation. As
soon as his financial circumstances
began to improve he began work on
the castle and was responsible for the
transformation of the Great Hall into

the Drawing Room with elegant
stucco-work on the vaulted ceiling
and the decoration of the Chapel
with painted wooden panels featuring
biblical scenes. Tradition has it that
in the left-hand corner at the back
sits the ghost of the Lady in Grey, an
unfortunate woman who died as the
result of a tragic love story.

128-129 The crypt has conserved its Medieval appearance. The walls are so thick as to be able to house a secret chamber. The furnishings in heavy oak combine well with the hunting trophies, arms and armor.

129 top left A copy of the beautiful portrait of the Queen Mother painted by De Lazlo when she was the Duchess of York hangs in her room. The names of the 14th Earl, his wife and his children are embroidered on the inside of the canopy.

129 right The chapel is the most beautiful room in the whole of the castle, with its walls and ceiling fully paneled in painted wood with sacred scenes, from the Last Supper to the Flight from Egypt, by the Dutch artist Jacob de Wet.

The Lady in Grey is not, however the only ghost to haunt the castle, being accompanied by the enormous and bearded figure of Earl Beardie who played cards with the devil and lost.

The opulent interiors belong to diverse periods from the fourteenth through to the nineteenth century, and contain collections of furniture, porcelain, paintings and historical objects.

The royal apartments are crammed with objects including photographs that document the relationships and the lives of the members of the family. The village of Glamis itself is composed of houses built in 1793 by the Earl of Strathmore for his estate workers.

These long, single-story constructions contain a schoolroom, a kitchen and a room for spinning and weaving wool.

SCONE PALACE

Although the massive stone palace on the banks of the Tay outside Perth dates from the first half of the nineteenth century, Scone is one of the oldest and most sacred sites in the whole of Scotland. Within the estate, in fact, rises Moot Hill, a place name deriving from the Gaelic *Tom-a-mhoid*, meaning "a place where justice is administered." It was here in 846 that Kenneth MacAlpine founded Celtic Abertha, the capital of the unified kingdom of the Scots and Picts. From that date onwards the Scottish kings were crowned on the consecrated Stone of Destiny, brought by MacAlpine from Dunstaffnage. Even when Edward I of England carried the stone to Westminster Abbey in London, where it was incorporated into the Coronation Throne, the Scottish kings continued to be crowned at Scone. On the same site around 1120, King Alexander I founded the first Augustinian monastery in Scotland. The abbey and the abbot's palace were also used as a residence by the royal family. The monastery complex enjoyed great prosperity during the reign of Robert III and the rising city of Edinburgh was annexed to the abbey so that it could benefit from its great wealth. In 1210 William the Lion founded a royal settlement a short distance away, on the site of what is today the city of Perth. On the 27th of June, 1559, the monastery was sacked by the fanatical followers of John Knox, inflamed by one of his sermons held at St. John Street in Perth.

132 top The Ambassador's Room is dominated by the purple four-poster bed carrying the coat of arms of King George III and the royal monogram. The bed was presented to Lord Stormont when he was the ambassador to the French court. On the walls hang a portrait of him by Allan Ramsay and another of Lady Elizabeth, the ambassador's daughter, with Dido the daughter of the chambermaid the Duke had freed from slavery.

132-133 The Long Gallery is in fact around 142 feet long, an unusual size for a Scottish house which were generally developed vertically.

The feet of many sovereigns have trodden the wooden floors inlaid with blackened peat bog oak. In 1580 the ceiling was frescoed with hunting scenes featuring James VI and his court, but was covered over at the beginning of the 19th century with a more sober Gothic-style ceiling.

The ruins of the royal town and the monastery, and the great estate surrounding them, became the property of the Earls of Gowrie who in the sixteenth century constructed Gowrie Palace using the stones of the old abbey. Following the obscure Gowrie Conspiracy in which James IV would have been killed had he not been rescued by Sir David Murray, the property of the Gowries reverted to the Crown. As a reward the estate was presented to the Murray family, of noble Flemish ancestry and future Earls of Mansfield. Early in the eigteenth century, the 5th Viscount David opposed the Act of Union and during the revolt of 1715 gave hospitality to James III, the Old Pretender, at Scone Palace. His son the 6th Viscount, in his turn opened the doors of

the palace to Bonnie Prince Charlie during the revolt of 1745. The viscount's brother William Murray became one of the greatest legal experts of the era and was invested as Earl of Mansfield. However, he lived in Bloomsbury, London, and was too busy to visit Scone. The 2nd Earl found the palace too damp and absolutely unsuitable for living in. It was not until the middle of the last century that the 3rd Earl commissioned the architect William Atkinson to construct a palace in the Neo-Gothic style, the building that can be admired today. Its massive external appearance with numerous lateral towers belies the wealth of the collections of French furniture, clock, tapestries, ceramics and ivory conserved inside.

DRUMMOND CASTLE

134 left and 135
In spite of the
modifications made
during the last
century, Drummond
Castle still retains
all the features of a
17th-century Scottish
Renaissance castle.
It is located on a rise
with terraces
dropping away
towards the gardens.

134 right
The garden's design
changed throughout
the centuries. One of
the artificers of the
Renaissance
transformation
of the castle and the
garden was John
Drummond, the 2nd
Earl of Perth who
lived between 1584
and 1662.

rummond Castle stands on a rocky outcrop, two miles out of Crieff in the heart of Perthshire. Around 1490, Sir John Drummond of Stobhall was given permission by James IV to construct a fortress on land that he had acquired in the Strahearn Hills. James IV, a frequent visitor to Drummond Castle, fell in love with Sir John's daughter, Margaret, but the Scottish noblemen were determined that their sovereign should marry the sister of the English king, Henry VIII and therefore poisoned the young Margaret.

In 1605, on the orders of James VI, the 4th Lord Drummond traveled to Spain with the delegation entrusted with the task of negotiating a peace treaty between the two nations. This enterprise earned him the title of Earl of Perth. The new earl had a wing added to the original tower on the north side. His brother John, the 2nd Earl of Perth, a privy counselor to James VI and Charles I, transformed the castle by adding a low Renaissance-style element between 1630 and 1636, as recorded in the dates incised together with the family coat of arms. The architect of the extension was John Mylne who was also responsible for the sundial obelisk standing in the center of the garden. During the period of suppression by the English army under the leadership of Cromwell, the castle was badly damaged. In 1715 it became a garrison for the troops faithful to the crown and after 1745 the lands of the

Earls of Perth, including Drummond Castle, were confiscated as punishment for their support of the Jacobite cause. Formal gardens in the Renaissance style are laid out at the foot of the castle and are considered to be the most beautiful in Scotland. Box hedges and examples of topiary create a play of light and shadow on the emerald lawns and gravel paths, while the rose garden and the flower beds lend splashes of color to the composition.

136 top Italian influences can be seen in the gardens at Drummond in the form of the statues, the fountains and the urns adorning the balustrades. It is thought that many statues were bought in Italy by Charles Barry around 1830.

136 bottom In September 1842 Queen Victoria stayed at Drummond Castle for three days and recorded in her diary: "Sunday, 11th September... We walked in the garden and it is really very fine with terraces, like an old French garden." The following day, while Prince Albert was hunting in the forest of Glen Artney, the queen strolled amidst the flowers accompanied by the Duchess of Norfolk.

136-137 and 137 top
From the upper terrace the garden appears in all its glory with the avenues and shrubs tracing the cross of St. Andrew with the 17th-century sundial at the center. Around the base, a mosaic of black and white pebbles forms the Drummond coat of arms.

Castles of Bavaria

SECTION TWO

138-139 Ludwig II of Bavaria's last dream was Herrenchiemsee Castle. The hundreds of candles used to illuminate it were lighted when the king was in the castle; he loved to wander about admiring his image reflected in the mirrors by the flickering, eerie candlelight.

B avaria's unconventional *status* within the Federal Republic of Germany is confirmed by the title that this *Land*, the largest and oldest of the sixteen *Länder* of Germany, uses when it proclaims its boundaries in official documents and signs: *Freistaat Bayern* (the Free State of Bavaria). In all of Germany, no one is as proud of their own uniqueness and independence as the Bavarians, a romantic and combative people that forged the history of Europe for centuries. Bavarians often express their loyalty in descending order: "First Bavaria, then Europe, and then Germany," and in fact they have every right to be proud of their land. Essentially, the only thing missing in its endless list of natural beauties is the sea. The great love that Bavarians have always had for their land can be seen in the respect they have traditionally accorded the countryside. All works by human hands, from the great art cities to rural villages, from imposing fortresses to opulent residences, and from little country churches to the magnificent monasteries, are harmoniously inserted, like jewels in a precious setting, into the multifaceted natural frame created by imposing mountain ranges dotted with emerald lakes, deep forests broken by meandering rivers, and gentle hills interrupted by large, crystal-clear lakes. Located in the heart of Europe, Bavaria's long history can be traced in the architecture of its monuments, echoing the influence of other peoples, wars and glories. The Celts, Romans, French and Austrians have all had their turn at dominating this territory, which takes its name from the Baiuvarii, the Germanic tribe that first settled here. Every culture left its mark on the countryside, in the culture and in the cuisine of Bavaria, but throughout its long, intricate history, the events which probably most affected its modern-day appearance were two major conflicts: the Thirty Years' War and the Second World War. The bigotry and persecution practiced by Catholics and Protestants during the Reformation finally erupted into one of the most devastating conflicts (both in terms of human life and artistic treasures) that Europe had ever known – the Thirty Years' War, which sucked France, Spain, Denmark and Sweden into its vortex of senseless violence.

140 top From the baroque gardens, the horseshoe-shaped staircase leads to the terrace where Linderhof Castle, Ludwig II's pleasant refuge in the valley of Graswang, stands.

140 bottom "Atlas Upholding the World" dominates the tympanum of Linderhof's main façade. The Kingdom of Bavaria's coat of arms, upheld by two winged spirits, appears in the tympanum.

140-141 Ludwig II began construction of Neuschwanstein Castle in 1848 in one of the most beautiful areas of Bavarian Allgaü-Swabia, with the idea of creating the castle of the Knights of the Holy Grail.

141 top In the park at Herrenchiemsee, fountains, geometrical hedges and statues depicting hunting scenes and mythological deities recreate the atmosphere of court gardens during the era of Louis XIV, the Sun King.

142 top left Prunn Castle, with its incredible position, overlooks the tranquil Altmühl River.

142 center left When new techniques of warfare made fortified defensive castles obsolete and the Renaissance breathed a new spirit of life throughout Europe, even the Bavarian nobles left their austere, uncomfortable

fortresses to build new palaces and residences with the luxuries of the new era. This photograph shows Nymphenburg Castle, the Wittelsbach family's summer residence.

142 bottom left The picture shows the Würzburg Residence. With their love for architecture and the fine arts, the von Schönborn family of bishop princes

embellished innumerable cities of Bavaria, including Neuburg, Bamberg and Würzburg.

142 top right Located in a picturesque setting and surrounded by water, Mespelbrunn Castle is a perfect example of a fortified structure which over the centuries was transformed into an elegant residence.

After the war, it took Germany forty years to recover from the resulting social and economic collapse (almost a third of the population had been killed). The Wittelsbach family, however, whose name runs like a thread throughout the history of Bavaria, embarked on the great task of rebuilding their land.

As the result of the long war, trading and communication difficulties and an even longer period of recovery, the whole country thus made the transition from the Gothic period directly to the Baroque, almost entirely skipping the Renaissance, which left only rare traces throughout most of Germany. In effect, the new style coming from Italy, so exuberant, rich and sensual, was the perfect antidote to sober Protestantism and all the ugliness of the preceding conflicts.

Newly regained economic well-being made it possible to invest in the best artists of the period, and cities, castles and churches were rebuilt and restored in the new style, adapted to local taste, thus creating the Bavarian baroque.

Unfortunately, in the heat of the moment almost everything that had survived the past catastrophes was made baroque, and even though many Romanesque and Gothic buildings have survived to the present, it is extremely rare to find interiors which were not modified in accordance with the taste of the times.

Unfortunately, World War II left an indelible scar, as Bavaria was one of the areas in Germany with the greatest wealth of artistic treasures. Yet it can still astound us with the uniqueness and variety of its natural beauties and historic monuments.

In this book we have chosen to show Bavaria through the history and images of its fortresses and castles, which function as both a point of departure and a point of arrival in the history of a particular area, town or city. World-renowned for the castles of Ludwig II, Bavaria truly is a land of castles.

There are hundreds of ruins, with fortresses, fortifications, and royal residences that emerge everywhere out of the idyllic countryside as witnesses to the long history of Bavaria, its desire for independence and freedom and its pride in and awareness of its accomplishments. It was difficult to select only a few of these castles, because they all have an individual charm and a unique architecture, interior or position that make them worthy of being added to the most representative groups. We thus decided to divide them into three chapters unrelated to itineraries (although the castles are described in geographical order from south to north), and connect them by historical and architectural groups instead.

The castles of Ludwig II have their own chapter, because they are really not part of the history and architecture of their period, but rather from some sort of dreamtime. The other two chapters are dedicated to fortified castles and residential castles.

142-143 *A true fortified citadel that for many centuries was an impregnable buttress guarding the borders of Lower Bavaria, Burghausen fortress, over 0.6 miles (1 km) long, is the longest fortified castle in Germany.*

143 top *The fortress of Nuremberg played an important role in the history of both Bavaria and Germany, and historically and architecturally is one of the most important fortresses in Europe.*

Neuschwanstein Castle.

Fränk. Saale

Coburg

Weisser Main

Aschaffenburg

Main

Main

Mespelbrunn

Bamberg

Roter Main

Bayreuth

Würzburg

Pottenstein

Aisch

Nuremberg

Naab

Ansbach

Altmühl

Regen

Riedenburg

Eichstätt

Prunn

Harburg

Danube

Isar

Danube

Augsburg

Landshut

Passau

Rott

Wertach

Amper

Isar

Lech

Scleissheim

Munich

Burghausen

Inn

Ammersee

Herrenchiemsee

Starnberger
See

Chiemsee

Kempten

Füssen   Hohenschwangau

Neuschwanstein

Linderhof

Herrenchiemsee Castle.

Schleissheim Castle.

Nymphenburg Castle.

146-147 Kaiserburg, one of the most beautiful and imposing fortresses in Germany, has undergone many changes over the centuries. Its massive Sinwell Tower can be seen for miles.

Harburg Castle.

Prunn Castle.

THE DREAM OF LUDWIG II, "THE FAIRY TALE KING"

Some of the most sumptuous and well-known castles in the world are certainly those of that symbol of Bavaria, Ludwig II, whose ministers consistently attempted to block their construction. These amazingly eccentric works were a product of the imagination and dreams of a monarch who was affectionately known as "The Fairy Tale King" by his subjects, but was considered the "Mad King" by his ministers. To understand his castles, one must look at the life of Ludwig II. He was very young when he inherited the heavy burden of a throne which had previously been occupied by two great political figures: his grandfather, Ludwig I, and his father, Maximilian II, who had succeeded in making Munich the European capital of art and culture. Born on August 25, 1845 in the royal palace of Nymphenburg in Munich, he passed a lonely adolescence in the manor of Hohenschwangau. His mother, queen Marie, notes in her diary that the child appreciated art, built churches and castles with his wooden blocks, liked to dress up and was very generous with his toys. This natural character and the type of education he received made him a dreamer. Fantastic images of the historical past, German sagas and a love of the exotic steadily distanced him from reality. As he grew up, he became enamored of the figure of the Sun King and the splendors of Versailles. His father's ideal of a constitutional monarchy was totally contrary to the vision of abso-

lute power and the passion for the Bourbons that had rooted in him. Another passion that caused no end of problems with his ministers was his love for Richard Wagner's music, which at that time was considered a hodgepodge of deafening sounds, discordant and even dangerous. As soon as he came to the throne, Ludwig II began to search for his hero, who had gone into hiding to avoid debts and had left his works incomplete. Thanks to the king's support and enormous monetary contributions, Wagner was able to complete his works, and his music gained international recognition. The veneration and love that the young Wittelsbach felt for the *maestro* were boundless, but unlike his grandfather, who preferred the love of Lola Montez to his reign, Ludwig did not have the necessary strength of character to oppose the orders of his Cabinet, which, worried about the "unbalancing" effect of Wagner's music and personality on the king, banished the artist from the court. The bond of affection between the brilliant composer and the restless monarch is evidenced in the letters the two exchanged, which in their exuberance and passion are not only some of the most revealing documents of the era, but are also a portrait of two unique, creative personalities. The great disappointment that this forced separation caused, besides continued opposition to his rare political decisions, caused him to distance himself even farther from politics and to lose himself in his world of dreams.

148 top left
This portrait by Franz von Lenbach shows an elderly Richard Wagner. The painting hangs in Herrenchiemsee Castle, although the temple that Ludwig dedicated to the composer is actually Neuschwanstein Castle.

148 bottom left
Young King Ludwig II of Bavaria looked like an ideal monarch to his people. Tall, slim and quite attractive, with a very elegant style and demeanor, his amiable nature won over any subjects who were fortunate enough to meet him.

148 right
Maximilian II rebuilt Hohenschwangau Castle in Romantic style. This summer residence stimulated the historical romanticism that spurred Ludwig II to build his fanciful castles.

149 Ludwig II of Bavaria, surrounded by the Wittelsbach dynasty, is shown in this Franz X. Thallmaier painting hanging in Herrenchiemsee Castle.

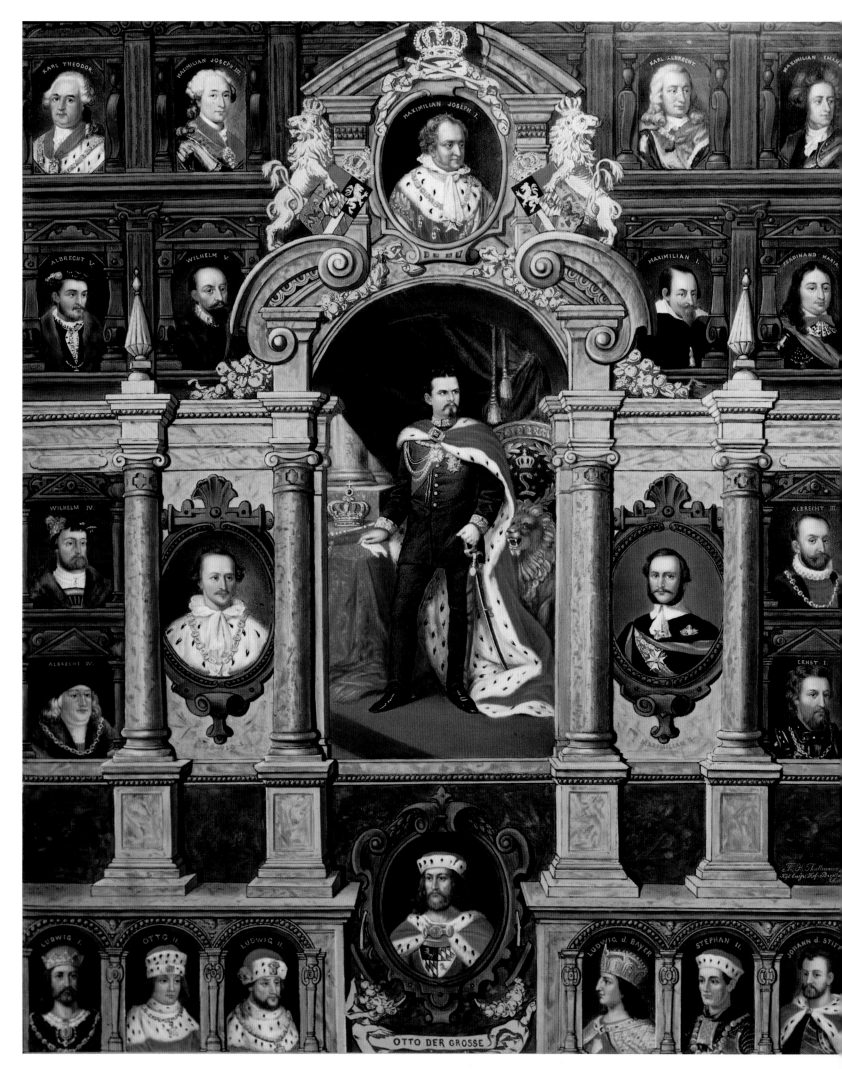

As he could not restore a rule of absolute power, he at least wanted to build a monument to himself. The resulting castles, which he himself designed and conceived, are the product of an unbridled imagination and a taste for the excessive and spectacular that only a king from times past could afford, combined with the period taste for mixing styles of past eras and the king's personal passion for German mythology and exotic settings. The

king was not so much a madman as he was an eccentric dreamer, with the power, position and money to satisfy his whims and make his imaginary realm a reality. He loved to dress in the costumes of his legendary heroes, and would depart on nighttime runs on his gilded sleigh, accompanied by his faithful mounted escort. His bizarre behavior accelerated along with his strange deeds, which became increasingly frenzied. All this fed the imagination of the people, who loved

his truly kingly excesses and adored him when, tall and handsome, he would come out of nowhere to share his lunch with a woodcutter, or knowledgeably discuss livestock with a shepherd. He was nevertheless quite shy and reserved and hated court occasions. He had very few friends, and the only woman in his life was his cousin Elizabeth, the empress of Austria, known as "Sisi." There was a deep platonic love between the two, who understood each other and shared confidences. Elizabeth was herself a strange character, and like the king was a great aesthete who was obsessed with her beauty. While Ludwig always carried his helmet under his arm so as not to crush his curls, the Austrian empress was obsessed with her weight and constantly engaged in physical activity and diets. Ludwig became engaged to Sisi's younger sister Sophie, perhaps to stop gossip about his relationship with Elizabeth, who was already the empress of Austria, or to put an end to more serious rumors about his homosexuality, but he broke off the engagement only 15 days before the wedding, when the sumptuous coach for the marriage had already been prepared. It is now on display at the Nymphenburg Museum, along with Ludwig's numerous other coaches. But it was neither scandals nor the king's eccentric behavior that finally prompted his ministers to place the king under judicial interdict, but rather his castles.

150-151 Like a magician's spell, the white pinnacles of Neuschwanstein Castle rise out of the early morning mist.

151 top Linderhof Castle, with its pale color and rounded façade, fountains and baroque garden covered with a blanket of snow, almost seems a natural part of the winter landscape.

*152 and 153
Schachen Castle,
built in the Alps near
Garmisch-
Partenkirchen, is
actually a rustic
mountain retreat
which Ludwig II
wanted for a
hunting lodge. It
nevertheless deserves
to be called
a castle because of its
interior, which with
the king's usual taste
for opulence stands
in sharp contrast to
the simplicity of the
exterior and is full
of gilt and flourishing
touches. Still, to
maintain a little
of the intimate and
cozy atmosphere of
a mountain refuge,
the monarch
furnished several
rooms, such as the
study (top right), the
dining room (center
right) and the
bedroom (bottom
right) in a more
simple and sober style.*

In order to build and decorate them, Ludwig had gone into debt and had taken out loans of millions of marks from the Bank of Bavaria, and Linderhof and Herrenchiemsee had almost been repossessed by creditors. Yet it was impossible to dissuade the king from what he considered his mission. Citing the pretext that there was a strain of madness on his mother's side of the family (whose brother Otto was epileptic), the Cabinet had the king declared mentally infirm by a team of psychiatrists, whose judgment was then certified by an eminent luminary of the time who never examined the patient personally. Ludwig II was placed under house arrest at the castle of Berg on Starnberg Lake. On July 13, 1886, at the age of 40, overweight and suffering from the effects of tranquilizers and alcohol, he and his physician were found drowned on the banks of the lake that had been the scene of his few happy moments with his beloved cousin.

There are many theories on his death – some say it was a suicide (but why would his doctor have committed suicide too?), or that he tried to flee and was drowned (but he was an excellent swimmer), or that he was murdered because he had become too inconvenient. Whatever the explanation, his death was tragic and senseless. The empress Elizabeth, who was perhaps the only one who understood his soul, made this comment upon Ludwig's death: "The king was not mad; he was only an eccentric who lived in a world of dreams. They should have treated him more gently..."; Paul Verlaine called him "the only true king of our century." The fruit of his romantic delirium, the castles of Neuschwanstein, Herrenchiemsee and Linderhof, spelled his disaster and his downfall but enriched the future of Bavaria with what are now the greatest tourist attractions not only in Bavaria, but in all of Germany.

NEUSCHWANSTEIN CASTLE

154 top This photo
shows a view from the
west side of the castle,
with its high
octagonal tower and
balcony inspired by
that of Wartburg
Castle.

154 bottom
Neuschwanstein's
brick entry is
a contrast to the
white winter
world.

155 Neuschwanstein
Castle emerges from
the mists and clouds
like a page in the
legend of the Holy
Grail.

Neuschwanstein was the first of three castles begun in 1869, but was the last to be completed in 1886. Ludwig II did not enjoy it for long. In June of that same year he was deposed and left this castle for his last "escorted" trip to Berg, where he met his end.

This fairy tale castle, which certainly inspired Walt Disney for his cartoons, was based on a childhood dream of the king that prompted him to create a utopian dwelling that would be both a medieval knights' castle and a temple to Wagner.

In his dream, the Swan Knight Lohengrin (in German *Schwan* means swan, which is why this creature recurs as a symbol and name) and the heroes of the Holy Grail spoke to him from the walls of Hohenschwangau Castle, while he eagerly gazed at the hill before it, hoping to capture the fleeting image of a true knight within the crumbling walls of the old medieval castle of Hinterschwangau. Wagner's music deeply touched Ludwig's mind and heart, but part of his attachment to the *maestro* was surely related to their mutual passion-obsession for German mythology. The period's romantic taste for restoring buildings in medieval style merged with his vision of the castle of the Swan Knight Lohengrin as he had seen him on the walls of his father's castle and heard him through the notes of Wagner's music. The astounding result of this dream was a castle so elaborate and perfect that it seems impossible to have been built by human beings using earthly materials, and more likely that divine hands placed it there overnight. Gleaming with a whiteness that stands out even from a distance, it seems to be resting on the treetops. Its five floors are interrupted by a myriad of towers, pinnacled turrets and columns that remind one of the sand castles children build by dribbling wet sand through their fingers.

While the exterior is enchanting, the interior is hypnotic: silks, brocades, lapis lazuli, gilt, bronze majolica, porcelains, marbles, and inlaid and engraved wood are used for all the architectural styles of the past – Gothic, Romanesque and Byzantine – but the sensation is never one of a hodgepodge, but rather the creation of yet another style, recognizable in all his Bavarian castles, which perhaps should be referred to as "Ludwigesque." Neuschwanstein Castle is perhaps the greatest example of 19th-century historicism, when Art Nouveau became the common thread joining the past eras that so greatly influenced the romantic spirit of the times.

What is more, all the king's projects made use of state-of-the-art techniques, with running water and complicated heating and special effects systems. Some stupendous examples include the grotto at Linderhof, the dinner table at Herrenchiemsee that can be raised and lowered through the floor to permit Ludwig to eat in solitude, and the kitchen at Neuschwanstein, ultra-modern for its time. While Maximilian II and Ludwig I built primarily for the public, the castles of Ludwig II were for himself alone.

They were his very life, places where dream and reality merged and history came to life. As he wrote in a letter to Wagner, "in an ideal, monarchic and poetic solitude," he had tried to create an art in harmony with his personal ideal of the universe.

156 The white and blue colors of Bavaria stand out on one of the coats of arms that decorate the windows of the corridor.

156-157 Upon suggestion by Wagner, Ludwig II went to visit Wartburg Castle near Eisenach, the historical setting for the singing contest in Tannhäuser. *The king was so impressed by the castle that he wanted to recreate many of its moods in Neuschwanstein.*

157 top The most beautiful view of the fairy-tale castle is from the Maria Bridge. In the background is the village of Füssen.

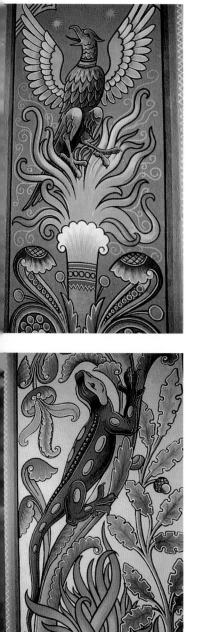

158 left This photo shows the details of one of the fanciful painted friezes that cover the walls of the Singers' Room.

158-159 and 159 top Two different angles of the Singers' Room show the beauty of the caisson ceiling, painted with

ornamental motifs and the signs of the zodiac, and the string of brass candelabras and candle holders for over 600 candles.

159 center
The Singers' Room ends with arcades of marble columns that frame a representation of the sorcerer Klingsor's wood. Above the arcades are paintings of other characters in the Legend of Parsifal, to whom the room is dedicated.

159 bottom
Paintings which portray moments in the life of the young Parsifal line the wall that runs along the corridor; this one recounts the episode in which the young hero meets and kills the Red Knight with his boy's sword.

160 top The saga of Gudrun, Sigurd's widow, who would marry Attila and then assassinate him, is portrayed on the walls of the Waiting Room of the Singers' Room.

160 bottom The central floor of the Throne Room is entirely in mosaic and includes ornamental forms and figures of plants and animals.

161 The two-level Throne Room is in the sumptuous style of a Byzantine church and is modeled after the All Saints' Church in Munich.

162 left top A painting depicting the meeting between Tannhäuser and Venus is shown on the walls of the King's Study.

162 top right A gilt bronze centrepiece depicting the battle between Siegfried and the Dragon stands on the richly inlaid table in the Dining Hall.

162 bottom left The symbol of the castle, a white swan, stands on the delicate majolica stove. The word Schwan *is in fact German for swan. The painting above depicts the arrival of Lohengrin.*

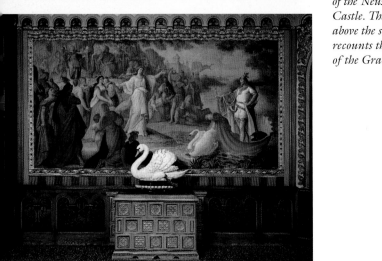

162 bottom right The Living Room is dedicated to the saga of Lohengrin, the Swan Knight, whose deeds charmed the young Ludwig and inspired the creation of the Neuschwanstein Castle. The mural above the sofa recounts the miracle of the Grail.

162-163 The Study is on the third floor, where the king's apartments are located; it is oak-paneled and filled with precious oak furniture. The ceiling is of inlaid wood and the saga of Tannhäuser is painted on the walls.

164 top These canvas paintings depict scenes described in the poetry of Walther van der Vogelweide and Hans Sachs.

164 center As in all his other castles, Ludwig wanted his bed chamber to be especially sumptuous. In contrast with the other rooms in Romanesque style, this room is in late Gothic style.
The silver swan ewer over the wash basin is noteworthy.
The painting on the walls are dedicated to the poem of Tristan and Isolde.

164 bottom
The windows of the Royal Dressing Room look out over the upper courtyard.
The violet silk curtains are embroidered with peacocks, a beloved and recurring symbol in Ludwig II's castles.

165 The King's Oratorium is paneled in oak with neo-Gothic ornamentation.
The paintings on the walls, the windows and the central triptych represent Saint Louis, Ludwig II's patron saint.

166 top left Murals in the Waiting Room of the royal apartments on the third floor recount the legend of Sigurd, whose saga corresponds to the medieval saga of Siegfried; the version recounted in the Edda is the most ancient collection of Germanic legends in existence. This painting shows Regin as he forges the famous sword Gram for young Sigurd.

166 bottom left The old wise man Gripy foretells young Sigurd's destiny.

167 This painting in the series painted by W. Hauschild in the Waiting Room of the Singers' Room, portrays King Attila courting Gudrun, Sigurd's widow.

166 right Using a sword forged by the dwarf Regin, Sigurd kills Fafnir, who in the guise of a dragon guards the treasure taken from the Nibelungen.

LINDERHOF CASTLE

168 top left
The majolica vases that adorn the eastern flowerbeds are of Nymphenburg make, copied from the originals from Choisy-le-Roi.

168 bottom left
The photo shows one of the two wrought iron nymphs pouring water into the little fountain at the foot of the first terrace on the main parterre in front of the palace.

The lovely Graswang Valley where Linderhof stands was a familiar place to the young Crown Prince. His father had already built a hunting lodge there, and when Ludwig II decided to build his Versailles, he originally planned it to be located near his castle at Linderhof. The original 1870 plan underwent many changes, and in the end Ludwig selected Lake Chiemsee for his Versailles project, building Herrenchiemsee Castle on an island in the lake. Linderhof, on the other hand, was designed to be a royal villa, while still keeping the look of Versailles. While it has been compared to the Petit Trianon and is decorated in eighteenth-century style, the castle's construction style is actually the only thing that resembles Versailles. It is the smallest of the three castles, with a more private, if not comfortable, touch. It is the only one of the three which the king saw to its conclusion in 1878, and where he lived most often and for the longest periods of time. The baroque and rococo interior is showy and ostentatious, full of gold and the brilliant blue which was the monarch's favourite color. Swans and peacocks, Ludwig's two favorite animals, are one of its recurrent themes, as at his other castles, but only here does the royal coat of arms of Bavaria appear, both on the façade and in the interior. Despite its majesty and splendor, it was not intended as a state building, but rather as a retreat. While Herrenchiemsee was an ode to Louis XIV and

168 top right Karl von Effner, the director of the Royal Court Gardens, created the artistic design for the gardens in the north and south portions of Linderhof, following the models of the Italian Renaissance. Before the castle, the water from the fountain with its gilt zinc "Flora and Putti," spurts up to 30 m high.

168 bottom right Right behind the palace, a little panoramic temple overlooks a flight of thirty marble steps. At its feet is the wrought-iron fountain of Neptune and a large flowerbed in the form of a Bourbon lily.

169 Linderhof Castle is a small, splendid structure in rococo style that is one of Ludwig II's most elegant creations.

171 top Behind the fountain entitled "Cupid Shooting His Arrows", a leafy pavilion protects the stone bust of Louis XVI, to whom Ludwig felt bound by a certain kinship, as the king of France had baptized Ludwig I, Ludwig II's grandfather and godfather.

Neuschwanstein a celebration of Wagner and his muses, Linderhof was where the king most clearly expressed his desire to retreat into his fantasy world, where he alone could be the actor and the audience. On the rises of the valley, around the central portion of the royal villa, the king built small structures that became his microscopic fantasy world. The Moorish pavilion and the Moroccan house exude the exotic atmosphere of *The Thousand and One Nights*; in the hunting lodge he could stretch out on animal skins and drink mead to become one of the deities of the Nibelungen; and the Venus Grotto became his Blue Grotto, where he sailed on a gilded, shell-shaped boat. The gardens provide a natural link between the rococo castle and the rugged majesty of the Alpine landscape. Following the example of the Italian Renaissance, he took advantage of the natural features of the terrain to build terraces and waterfalls that allowed the flowerbeds and English gardens to blend into the natural mountain setting.

*170 top left
The eastern parterre includes four semirectangular flowerbeds that surround a quatrefoil pond. In the centre is a gilt group of statues entitled "Fame", at the back of the garden is the "Cupid with Dolphins," the central group of another small fountain. A terra-cotta bust of Louis XIV, whom Ludwig II considered an ideal absolute monarch, can be seen in the pavilion that closes off the garden.*

*170 bottom left
The photo shows one of the innumerable limestone statues that adorn the gardens.*

*170 top right
The golden statue entitled "Fame" rises above the four-leaf clover-shaped fountain in the western parterre.*

170-171 The gilt zinc cupid in the fountain in the eastern parterre seems to be shooting one of his arrows toward Linderhof's east façade.

172 top left
The Moorish pavilion
was built by the
Berlin architect Karl
von Diebitsch for the
international Paris
Exposition in 1867.
Ludwig II bought it
for Linderhof's park
and had it rebuilt
and refurnished,
making changes that
satisfied his taste for
opulence.

172 bottom left
As described for the
set in the first act
of The Valkyrie, *here*
is the Hunting Hut,
where the king could
sink into the
mythological world
of his heroes in
The Ring of the
Nibelungen.

172 right
The magically
illuminated area
of Venus' Grotto is
a reproduction of
the inside of
Hörselberg, the scene
of the first act of
Wagner's
Tannhäuser, *but the*
pool illuminated
from below draws its
inspiration from the
Blue Grotto at
Capri.

173 The king of
Bavaria's passion
for the exotic was
completely gratified
in the "Thousand
and One Nights"
atmosphere of the
Peacock Room in the
Moorish Pavilion.
The tails of the
enamelled wrought-
iron peacocks are
studded with
hundreds of
Bohemian glass stones.

174-175 A product of the cooperation between the architect Georg Dollmann and the set painter Joseph de la Paix, the model for the Room of Mirrors at Linderhof was the Mirror Room in the Rich Rooms of the Munich Residence.

175 top The theme of the Music Room is "The Courtly Festivals," as shown in the large canvas paintings by H. von Pechmann, which depict pastoral and social scenes. The group of stucco putti above the doors are signed by Schmidt.

175 bottom Like Herrenchiemsee, Linderhof Castle is richly furnished. The passion for exquisitely made objects and furniture made Ludwig II a true patron of his time for artists and craftsmen from both Germany and abroad. The clock in the photo is Swiss, and the vases are of Meissen porcelain.

176 Despite the intimate, cozy nature that Ludwig desired for Linderhof, he was unable to resist adding the central halls for court ceremonies, because he thought they were visual proof of an absolute monarchy. In the Audience Room there are in fact clear references to the kingdom of Bavaria in the stucco lunettes and above the throne's baldachin.

176-177 The painting on the left back wall of the Music Room is entitled "Pair of Shepherds at the Fountain," while that on the right is "Shepherd Girls with Bagpipe Player." The musical instrument is an aeolodion, *a combination of a piano and a harmonium.* In the centre is a life-size painted Sèvres porcelain peacock.

177 top The paintings in the East Tapestry Room, like those in the Music Room, were done on rough canvas to give a tapestry effect. The dark door frames are not ebony, but a special black marble from Belgium.

177 bottom A two-winged staircase, a smaller version of the Ambassadors' Stairway at Versailles, leads to the upper floor. In the center is a Sèvres vase which Emperor Napoleon III is said to have given to Ludwig II.

*178-179
A triumph
of luxury,
Herrenchiemsee
Castle rises out
of a dense wood
on Herreninsel,
the largest island
on Lake Chiemsee.*

*178 top The façade
of the castle can be
seen among the sprays
of water from the
fountains. The castle
is even more
sumptuously
furnished than its
model in France.*

*L*udwig's last great and most ambitious plan was to build a palace that was a replica of Versailles. His dream was to build the royal palace on the site of a modest hunting lodge built by his father near Linderhof, and over a period of five years the architect Georg Dollmann submitted thirteen designs for this "Meicost Ettal" (an anagram for "L'état c'est moi," the motto of Louis XIV). In 1873, based on the last design, which exceeded the original Versailles in size, Ludwig decided to build the palace on the island of Herrenchiemsee on Lake Chiemsee, just a few miles north of Munich. He did not simply copy the French royal palace, but used it as a model for the most typical portions of the structure: the façade, the Ambassadors' Stairway and the king's state apartment. While Versailles is a conglomerate of structures from different periods, Herrenchiemsee was immediately conceived as a unitary system. Based on antique engravings, the Ambassadors' Stairway, which had been demolished in France in 1752, was reconstructed in Ludwig's palace and inserted symmetrically in its two wings.

The façade is larger than that of Versailles, and the Hall of Mirrors and rooms are also larger than the original. The sumptuous baroque bedchamber is different from the original, as is the so-called Small Apartment, a series of rooms not part of the original Versailles.

179 top The Fountain of Latona is a copy of the original at Versailles. The Statue of Latona overlooks the steps, where there are peasants transformed into frogs, with cast lead turtles and amphibians farther down.

179 bottom The great Fountain of Fame, a copy of a fountain in San Idelfonso in Spain, overlooks the north pond. There are numerous mythological and allegorical figures in cast lead both on the rock and on the edge of the pond.

180 top The oval windows in the frieze area have given the second antechamber its name, the so-called Oeil de Boeuf Room, which is similar to that at Versailles. There is a small bronze statue of Louis XIV in the middle of the room. The paintings on the walls are also dedicated to the Sun King.

180 bottom The great hanging lamp with 108 candles, the centerpiece, the vases and the clocks of the Dining Hall are all in Meissen porcelain. As at Linderhof, due to the king's excessive sense of privacy, the table was lowered down through the floor and sent back up after it was set and prepared.

181 In the Vestibule, divided by columns and pillars, on an extraordinary floor of colored marble, stands a monumental vase of Italian marble, with a pair of peacocks in bronze and translucent enamel. Along with the swan, the peacock was Ludwig II's emblem.

182-183 The Hall of Mirrors, based on a design by Georg Dollmann, is 98 m long, even longer than the one at Versailles. Ludwig II tried to bring the Galerie des Glaces back to its full splendor by reconstructing furnishings that had been lost for centuries.

These rooms were designed in Louis XV style, in an intentional contrast with the other rooms. The difference in style of the rooms is also due to the fact that the architect changed; Dollmann finished the state rooms and staircase in 1881, and in 1884 Julius Hofman took over to complete the king's rooms. Another significant difference is that at Versailles the rooms have no furniture, as it was destroyed and stolen during the revolution, while Herrenchiemsee is fully furnished.

As he had no models to imitate, all the furniture, porcelain, curtains, bronzes and clocks are original creations of the architects (whose designs the king himself often corrected and

completed), who could indulge in their creative fancies through the skilled artisans of Munich. Seven years of work were necessary on the parade chamber bed alone. Herrenchiemsee Castle should not be considered incomplete; even its original 1870 plan did not provide for any rooms within it other than those which are complete today. In order to celebrate his "absolute monarchy," all Ludwig needed or wanted were the rooms of Versailles. Herrenchiemsee is not a residence, but a monument, a stage for the works of a king who was born too late and could play his role only in fantasy, on an island that could be reached only by boat, far from the banalities of life.

*184 center left
A detail of the
"Astronomy and
History" panel shows
a putto holding up
a medallion with a
portrait of Ludwig
II. This is the only
such panel in the
whole castle, because
the doors were not
completed until after
the king's death.*

*184 top and 184-185
The fireplace in the
Porcelain Room is
of Tunisian marble.
The mirror, the
hanging lamp, the
candelabras, the
vases, the clocks and
the splendid console
tables with delicately
painted putti are all
in precious Meissen
porcelain.*

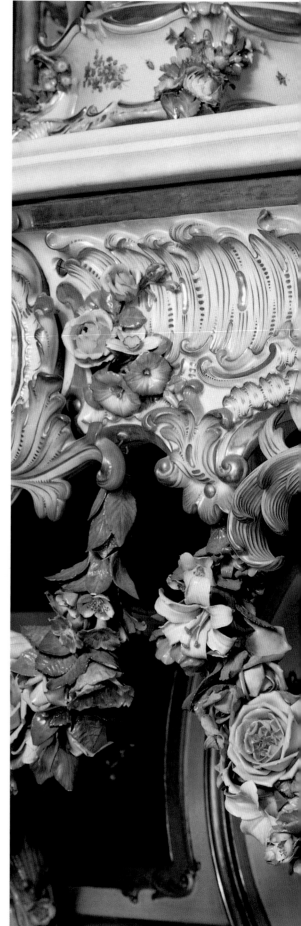

*184 bottom This
photo shows the
Porcelain Room. The
ceiling is stuccoed,
with a fresco
representing the Spirit
of Art. The precious
desk is made of
rosewood, with
painted Meissen
porcelain surfaces.*

*184 center right
This is another
detail of the room,
showing one of the
paintings with a
mythological theme
that duplicate the
originals hanging in
a room at
Fontainebleau
Palace.*

186 center left
In this painting by Ludwig Behringer (1864), the king is shown on horseback surrounded by his officials.

186 bottom
The halberds of the king's bodyguard are displayed amid the marble busts of the Sun King's marshals. The Bodyguard Room is modeled after the Salle des Gardes, *and along with two other antechambers, the Bed Chamber, the Council Room and the Hall of Mirrors, it is one of the state rooms which were not part of the king's residence.*

186 top The walls in the Hall of Peace are of marbleized colored stucco. A portrait of Louis XIV can be seen above the green Spanish marble fireplace. One of Herrenchiemsee's peculiarities is the oak floors with ornamental rosewood marquetry.

186 center right
The monumental staircase is modeled after the Ambassadors' Stairway at Versailles, which was demolished in 1752. The colored marble and marbleized stucco walls are a faithful duplication of the original, while the stairway at Versailles did not have the glass ceiling. The stucco figures in the niches were to have been of Vipiteno marble. Every time Ludwig came to the castle, the stairway was transformed into a carpet of flowers.

187 The Small Gallery ends the series of rooms that make up the royal apartments. The rooms are based on the Small Gallery at Versailles, which no longer exists. There are allegorical stucco figures in the niches and above the main cornice.

188 center Louis XIV was known for using his bed chamber for the first and last audiences of the day. The sumptuous State Room, which Ludwig II never used, is Herrenchiemsee at its most opulent.

188 bottom
The overflowing Blue Room is totally covered with relief decorations of gilt birds in iridescent colours. Mirrors are inserted into the panels so that the room seems to repeat itself endlessly.

188-189 Ludwig II's favourite color, blue, is used for the baldachin, the curtains and the silk and velvet coverings inlaid with gold in the King's Bed Chamber. The headboard of the sumptuous inlaid wood bed depicts the sun that symbolized Louis XIV. A blue ball used to illuminate the room at night stands on a gilt stand with beautiful inlay work.

188 top Luxury abounds in the King's Study as well, which is furnished with rare and priceless objects which are masterpieces of artistic craftsmanship. The great roll-top desk is a copy of the famous Bureau du Roi on display at the Louvre. The spectacular silver and gilt bronze Elephant Clock stands on one console table along with two other elaborate astronomical clocks.

SUMPTUOUS RESIDENCES FOR BAVARIAN NOBLES

As the dark years of the Middle Ages drew to a close, albeit much more slowly than in southern Europe, the scent of the Renaissance managed to permeate even Germany. Bavaria, with a spirit more akin to southern Europe than to the rest of the country, absorbed it quickly. Its cramped fortresses made it impossible to live comfortably, and the need for comfortable quarters suitable for entertaining had grown so rapidly that princes and nobles found it impossible to live in those damp old fortifications, which by now had become useless as a means of defense against more modern techniques of war. The Thirty Years' War interrupted the construction of residences more in line with aristocratic needs, but the 17th century marked the advent of residential castles and dwellings. The rivalry among the various nobles families, among the families of bishop princes, and between bishops and the nobility exploded in a race to see who could build the most sumptuous, ostentatious dwelling. The architectural style in fashion in Italy – opulent, theatrical and fanciful – was the perfect response to the ferment that was enlivening the souls of Bavarian nobles. Counts, dukes and bishop princes began to build airy palaces (in total contrast to the dark, cramped rooms of defensive fortresses) in or near the cities, with entire suites of rooms and richly furnished salons surrounded by fairy-tale parks with enchanting additional structures, such as *orangeries*, pavilions and little temples. Baroque taste spread in all new buildings (and in most of the old ones too), followed by a lighter, more airy and even more whimsical rococo. Thus, residential castles appeared at the dawn of the modern era, united by their style of magnificent showiness, but each with the personal imprint of those who wanted to leave a permanent mark of their power and fame.

191 top *Located among the forests and vineyards of Steigerwald, the splendid baroque palace of Pommersfelden is entirely decorated with elaborate frescoes. Its elegant architecture is still almost completely intact. The palace was built around the same time as the Würzburg Residence and the Neue Residence (New Residence) of Bamberg.*

THE MUNICH RESIDENCE

The superb Residence stands on the central Max Josef Platz, where it was built on order of Maximilian I and his son Ludwig I. Once the family home of the Wittelsbach family, it is now one of the most splendid museums of the world. When the Swedes conquered Munich during the Thirty Years' War, King Gustav Adolf, admiring the Residence, is said to have murmured, "If only it had wheels!" The Swedes not only did not carry it off, but their king's admiration for the splendid royal palace saved it from serious damage. Today, the Residence is considered one of the most beautiful Renaissance palaces in Europe, although the buildings that crowd around the seven inner courtyards date from the 16th to 19th centuries and are a mixture of all the different styles that alternated during those centuries: Renaissance, baroque, rococo and neoclassical. After the bombardments of the Second World War, the complex had to be almost entirely rebuilt, but most of its sumptuous furnishings were saved and have now been returned to their original positions in the rooms. The sections open to the public constitute the *Residenzmuseum*. The *Alte Residenz*, with its entrance on Residenzstrasse, contains the main court sectors, including the splendid *Altes Residenztheater*, the rococo jewel of architect François de Cuvilliés. The *Königsbau*, with its Renaissance façade built in imitation of the Palazzo Pitti, was commissioned by Ludwig I and now serves as the entry to the Residenzmuseum.

192 top The Residenz, the Wittelsbach family's residential palace, is considered one of the most beautiful Renaissance palaces in Europe, even though the buildings that stand around seven inner courtyards are a combination of Renaissance, rococo and neoclassical styles. The façade on Max

Joseph Platz was built between 1826 and 1833 by Leo von Kleuze, using the Palazzo Pitti and the Palazzo Rucellai as models.

192 center Between 1581 and 1586, Duke Wilhelm V ordered the building of the Grottenhof, *a structure with four wings and a richly*

decorated inner garden. Despite changes made, this "garden of secret delights" still exudes the joyous spirit of the Renaissance gardens of southern Europe.

192 bottom The Cave Room, covered in volcanic lava studded with shells, crystals and coloured rocks, opens onto the Grottenhof.

192-193 The Brunnenhof, or Court of Fountains, is a long octagon which was created between 1612 and 1616 by joining new buildings to already existing sections. The Wittelsbach Fountain, which stands in the center, honors the first duke of the dynasty, Count Otto von Wittelsbach, whose bronze statue is upheld by the four elements and the four river deities.

193 top This photo shows the south façade of the Residence, with the statue of Max Joseph Denkmal in the foreground. Unfortunately, what we see of the Residenz today is mostly a faithful reconstruction: the bombardments of 1945 destroyed this masterpiece of five centuries of Bavarian history in just a few hours.

The more recent north wing – built between 1837 and 1842 and known as the *Festsaalbau* – contains the *Herculessaal*, now a concert hall. The *Hofgarten*, a magnificent courtyard garden, was embellished during the reign of Maximilian I with porticoes and a little round temple with an interesting frescoed cupola.

The oldest portions of the palace are the *Grottenhof*, built under Wilhelm V in 1585 as a "garden of secret pleasures," and the *Antiquarium* (ordered by Albrecht V in 1568 to hold the Wittelsbach collection of antiquities), the work of Jacopo Strada and the most important Renaissance period secular construction north of the Alps. The most spectacular and extravagant rooms of the royal palace are on the upper floor. The *Reiches Zimmer* represent another splendid piece of German rococo by François de Cuvilliés, decorated with stucco work by Johann Baptist Zimmermann. They lead to the Secret Chapel, a niche gleaming with gilt and lapis lazuli decorations, with floors and walls covered with mosaics of marble and colored stone.

194 center The wall decorations in the Throne Room are astonishing and unique: the walls below the marbleized stucco panels are totally gilt with a network of palm-shaped decorations.

194 bottom The Imperial Room measures is 34x15 m and is 10 m high. The central paintings on the ceiling, which burned in 1944, have been replaced by scale-model photographic reproductions. The paintings above the windows were done in Venice by Andrea Vicentino. Fifteen wool tapestries depict heroes of the Old Testament.

194-195 The Reiche Kapelle *concludes the sequence of Rich Rooms in the Residence. The ceiling is decorated in gilt stucco work on an azurite background. Many scagliola decorations, the altar, the eight windows, and numerous reliquaries and statuettes were saved from the bombardments.*

195 top The Altes Residenztheater, or Cuvilliés Theatre, is the rococo triumph of the great Belgian architect and former court jester François de Cuvilliés. The Elector Max Emanuel discovered the dwarf's talent for design as soon as he arrived at court, and sent him to Paris to study.

SCHLEISSHEIM CASTLE

198 top left Duke Wilhelm V began construction of Old Schleissheim Castle in order to create a refuge from the responsibilities of the realm. In 1616 his son Maximilian I transformed it into an Italian Renaissance-style palace.

198 top right Little Lustheim castle, amidst its lovely French gardens, is about 30 years older than the New Castle. It was designed by Enrico Zuccalli and was built as a wedding present for Maria Antonia, the Elector's wife.

198-199 In 1701 the Elector Max Emanuel began work on New Schleissheim Castle, a monumental baroque palace that became the summer residence for the Electors of Bavaria.

199 The scagliola decorations and marbleized stucco work give the New Castle's chapel an embroidered effect. The gilt stucco work on the ceiling frames the opening to an upper level.

Schleissheim Castle is located in Oberschleissheim, about 20 miles from central Munich. This splendid baroque complex consists of two palaces built one in front of the other. The first, known as the Old Castle, was begun in 1597 as a modest residence for Duke Wilhelm V, based on a design by Heinrich Schön. In 1616 his son, Duke Maximilian I, took it over, and the "refuge" grew into an Italian Renaissance-style palace. Unfortunately, today's structure is only a pale shadow of what it was before the bombardments of World War II destroyed it. Only the outside has been reconstructed, but inside you can still admire an interesting exhibit of "domestic" religious objects like Nativity cradles, representations of the Passion and Easter eggs from eastern Europe.

The Old Castle is obscured by the grandiose New Castle. As early as 1693, the Elector Maximilian II Emanuel decided to expand the existing residence. The work was first directed by Enrico Zuccalli. The War of Spanish Succession put a stop to work until 1719, and Joseph Effner (a Bavarian architect who had studied in France) was commissioned to continue with the project following new plans. Effner hired great names in the architecture of the time, including François de Cuvillés, Johann Baptist Zimmermann and Cosmas Damian Asam, who became involved in a frenetic whirl of creativity. The New Castle was completed between 1847 and 1848, but the connection to the Old Castle which was to have completed the whole structure was never finished. Without counting the galleries and side pavilions, the main building's façade alone measures fully 1082ft (330 m) in length and is covered with precious late baroque ornamentation.

From the opulent ground floor, completely decorated in stucco work and frescoes and dotted with red marble columns, a magnificent staircase leads to the first floor where the *Barockgalerie* contains the most important collection of baroque paintings in Germany.

Even surrounded by all this magnificent baroque art, the *Grosser Saal* still takes the breath away, with a dazzling splendour only slightly dimmed by the superb paintings of Jacopo Amigoni that cover the ceiling with scenes from the history of the Wittelsbach family. The wonderful summer concerts of Schleissheim take place in this hall.

The elegant, French-style gardens, which are absolutely idyllic and a perfect setting for the buildings, are adorned by arabesques of a variety of flowers and colored rocks, geometrical hedges and canals with waterfalls. They were embellished by Joseph Effner and Dominique Girard in 1715. Within them rises *Gartenschloss* Lustheim (the Garden Palace), a lovely little castle built as a wedding gift for Maria Antonia, the wife of the prince. It was designed by Zuccalli as well. Its light, delicately decorated rooms contain one of the most beautiful collections of porcelain in Europe, the Meissner-Porzellansammlung, which blends in superbly with the baroque interior.

200 The large
Tapestry Room is
covered with precious
silk tapestries
depicting battle
scenes. The wooden
furniture is carved
and gilded, and the
porcelain objects
are of Nymphenburg
make.

201 Following the Sun
King's custom of
holding his first and
last audiences of the
day in the bed
chamber, a State Bed
Chamber was also
prepared at
Schleissheim, with an
alcove covered in silk
and velvet interwoven
with gold thread.

202-203 The elegant profile of the New Castle stands out against the clear sky of Bavaria. Rich furnishings and the Art Gallery, with works from the 16th to 18th centuries, give an idea of 18th-century court life.

Magnificent Nymphenburg Castle at the gates of Munich was the summer residence of Bavarian royalty until 1918. The spacious complex, whose most noteworthy feature is the large group of separate buildings connected by an absolute symmetry of line, is the result of various phases of work. Its development over the centuries is the result of the creativity of four generations of Wittelsbachs. The oldest part of the palace, the five-story central pavilion, was built in 1662 by Prince Ferdinand Maria, when his wife, Adelaide of Savoy, gave birth to his heir after 10 years of hopes in vain. The sumptuous edifice was designed by the Italian architect Agostino Barelli. Subsequently, the central portion of the palace and the magnificent double stairway at the entrance were designed by Enrico Zuccalli. Adelaide's son Max Emanuel inherited the castle, and in 1704, with the aid of Joseph Effner, he added the final touches that give the palace its present-day appearance: two Italian-style side villas, joined to the two wings of the main building, the court stables, the waterfall in the park, and the *Badenburg*, *Pagodenburg* and *Magdalenenklause* pavilions. During the reign of Karl Albrecht VII, the little villas for court nobles were built around the artificial lake in the courtyard facing the palace; since 1747 they have housed the famous Nymphenburg Porcelain Factory. In the park is the stupendous *Amalienburg*, a hunting lodge the Emperor ordered in honor of his wife Amalia.

204 top This photo shows a detail of the façade of the central pavilion at Nymphenburg, remodeled by the Elector Max Emanuel using late French baroque ornamental motifs.

204 bottom The photo is a view of the Rondell Bauten. Effner's design enlarged the palace by adding a vast semicircular cour d'honneur *in front of the main building. It was designed to include the Elector's stables and apartments for officials. Cuvilliés was responsible for executing the design, working under Karl Albrecht.*

204-205 The oldest part of Nymphenburg Castle is the central pavilion with its five floors. The old summer home had been built in 1664 by Adelaide of Savoy, the wife of the Elector Ferdinand Maria. The romantic princess dedicated the palace to the goddess Flora as "a place for recreation and pastoral pleasures."

205 top The Magdalenenklause pavilion consists of false ruins with feigned poverty meant to imitate the cells of hermits. Built in the middle of the park, it represents a desire to take refuge in solitude and escape formal court life.

206 and 206-207
Classical art and
feminine beauty were
the two great passions
of Ludwig I, Ludwig
II's grandfather.
To pay homage
to the women
in his life, the king
commissioned Joseph
Stieler to paint them
in 36 marvelous
portraits displayed
in the Gallery of
Beauties. The portraits
show the following

women in all their
splendor: Lady
Theresa Spencer (top
left), Caroline von
Holnstein (bottom
left), Marie of Prussia,
mother of Ludwig II
(top right), Helena
Sedelmayer, daughter
of a shoemaker
(center right), the
famous adventuress
Lola Montez (bottom
right) and Sophie von
Österreich, Ludwig I's
half-sister.

François de Cuvilliés, with the help of stucco work by Johann Baptist Zimmermann and wood decorations by Joachim Dietrich, ensured that even the splendor of the castle's Hall of Mirrors would pale in comparison with the interior of *Amalienburg*.

Maximilian Joseph III further embellished the palace, changing and redecorating many rooms. He also made use of the genius of Zimmermann and the elderly Cuvilliés, and gave the *Steinerner Saal* (Marble Hall) that sumptuous atmosphere that still enchants the spectators who come to summer concerts at Nymphenburg.

Another fascinating room is the extraordinary Gallery of Beauties, a collection of thirty-six portraits of the most beau-

tiful women of the period, painted by Joseph Stieler on commission by Ludwig I. Like his son and grandson, Ludwig I had great aesthetic taste, and like his grandson, his love of beauty caused him to lose his realm.

While Ludwig II's battles with his Cabinet were due to his castles, Ludwig I's problems in governing were due to the beauties of his gallery. Lola Montez, an adventuress of common origins, may not have been the most beautiful of the women in the portraits, but she was certainly the most intelligent. She had great political and personal influence over the king, whose government forced him to exile her. Thereafter, Ludwig I fell into a deep depression and abdicated in 1848.

207 top left
*The splendid effect
of this party room,
the* Steinerner Saal,
*is the result of Effner's
skilled use of space,
with walls broken
by pillars that support
the almost square
vault. During the
reign of Maximilian
Joseph III, Cuvilliés
divided the part
overlooking the
garden into two floors.
The frescoes were
done by the 76-year-
old Johann Baptist
Zimmermann.*

207 top right
*The Gallery of
Beauties is in the
former Small Dining
Room in the
apartments of Queen
Caroline, the wife
of Max Joseph I.
The gallery contains
portraits of not only
noblewomen, but
women of every social
level, bound only by
their special allure.*

210-211 The park of the Castle was significantly expanded in the 18th century following the fashion of French-style gardens. During the next century, the park was again remodeled according to the tenets of the English-style.

210 and 211 top left The Marstallmuseum building, where a superb collection of gala coaches from the Wittelsbach family is housed, is located south of the Nymphenburg complex. Some of its most precious pieces include the coaches and sleighs of Ludwig II, with the spectacular coach the king had built for his marriage to Sophie, Sisi's sister; the marriage was called off and the coach was never used.

211 top right In the restful atmosphere of the Pagodenburg Living Room, the white and blue color scheme of the Dutch tiles that cover the walls is repeated on the floor, in the paintings on the ceiling and in the furniture.

211 center right The pavilions of the princely summer residence were intended to provide a place of seclusion from incessant court activities, as well as exotic atmospheres that would give the impression of being in distant lands. On the outside, the Pagodenburg is simple, almost austere, but its interior is richly furnished for exclusive parties and exudes an atmosphere of the far-off Orient.

211 bottom right The three rooms on the upper floor of the Pagodenburg are decorated with Oriental motifs. This is one of the Chinese Rooms, with black lacquered panels and painted silk and rice paper.

ANSBACH CASTLE

Ansbach, a pearl of baroque and rococo style, is the capital of Rangau, the central region of Franconia, on the border of the Land of Baden-Württemberg. The city grew up within the Benedictine monastery founded by St. Gumbert in 748. In 1381, the city was taken over by the Burgraves of Nuremberg, the Hohenzollern family, who used it to extend the dominion of Ansbach-Bayreuth. A little later, it was chosen as the residence of one of the dynastic branches, and a splendid fortress on water was built there as the residence of the Von Brandeburg-Ansbach Margraves. The palace then underwent many renovations, until it was decided to build an entirely new residence.

In 1705 the architect Gabriel de Gabrieli (a native of Rovereto, Italy) was hired, but ten years later he left the job, which was continued by Leopoldo Retti of Como. The Margrave died, and the task of completing the ambitious work passed on to his widow. She expanded the original plan and created the park, the *Hofgarten* (Court Garden), where in memory of her husband she planted two rows of linden trees in the form of a cross. The magnificent Orangerie is located at the entrance to the gardens; today it is used as a concert hall. It was built in 1726 based on the model of two French architectural masterpieces: the side facing the gardens was inspired by the Grand Trianon at Versailles, while the other side was based on the Louvre. The gardens were also the scene of a dark and strange story, with a small stone marker showing the spot where, in 1883, Kaspar Hauser, a mysterious foundling inexplicably adopted by a rich English lord, was beaten to death for no apparent reason. The interior is in early rococo style, with delicate forms and colors. The *Festsaal* is extremely beautiful, embellished with stucco work and frescoes by Diego and Carlo Carlone, as are the brilliant *Spiegelkabinett* (Hall of Mirrors) and the priceless *Gekachelter Saal*, covered with 2800 ceramic tiles from Ansbach.

212 top The elegant façade of the Ansbach Residence, crowned by a balustrade with statues and gracefully dotted with pillars, is the work of Gabriel de Gabrieli and Leopoldo Retti.

212 bottom Every important noble residence of the period had to have an opulent Hall of Mirrors. The Spiegelkabinett of the Ansbach Residence was designed by J.C. Wezler in 1739, and in accordance with the baroque taste of the time is full of gilt and porcelain.

212-213 The Court Gardens lie to the southwest of the Residen. At the entrance is the great Orangerie, based on the Grand Trianon of Versailles. The building, more than 100 m long, is now used as a concert hall.

213 top One of the most noteworthy rooms in the Residence is the Party Room, designed in 1737 by Leopold Retti. Its refined stucco work was done by one of the most important stucco artists of the time, Diego Carlone.

The 820-ft (250-m) ceiling of the two-story room features an allegorical fresco by Carlo Carlone adulating the Margrave Carl Wilhelm Friederich, in the "good government" style thematized throughout art history.

214 top In the center of the large square, dominating the main entrance to the Residence, is the Franconia Fountain, with statues of great men of the region, including the sculptor Tilman Riemenschneider (right) and Matthias Grünewald, a painter, architect and hydraulic engineer (left).

THE WÜRZBURG RESIDENCE

214-215
The magnificent
Residence complex
consists of a central
structure and two
side wings. A
masterpiece
of German Baroque,
the lordly residence
was built between
1719 and 1744 based
on a design by
Balthasar Neumann,
with the assistance of
Lukas von
Hildebrandt from
Vienna and M. V.
Welsch from Mainz.

W ürzburg is a lovely city located in a splendid position on the Main River, surrounded by hills covered with vineyards that reach the city center. Its elegant eighteenth-century appearance survived the destruction of the Second World War, and its pearl is the Residence, the most beautiful baroque castle in all of Germany, located in the eastern portion of the city. In 1720 the new bishop prince, Johann Philipp von Schönborn, decided that it was time to build a palace which was larger and more modern than the massive fortress of Marienberg, perched on the hill. By this time, it was no longer necessary to live in a fortified castle, and after the Thirty Years' War the city was experiencing a period of economic growth and had a great desire to rebuild and renovate. The Schönborns were a rich and influential family which had produced at least twelve bishops, all with a passion for building and the gift of good taste. Johann Philipp demonstrated incredible far-sightedness in selecting Balthasar Neumann as his chief architect. This young man who built cannon and bells and until then had designed only his own home, became one of the greatest German architects of his time, and thanks to his genius, the bishop prince realized his dream of building a "castle to excel all other castles," a grandiose sandstone building soaring up splendidly from its own square. A half a century later, Napoleon called it the most beautiful residence in Europe.

215 top This portrait of Balthasar Neumann hangs in the Main and Franconia Museum in the Marienberg fortress. In the background one can see his masterpiece, the Residence. The Bohemian architect is shown in armor, resting on a cannon, as he was a gunner in the Episcopal artillery: architecture was only a hobby.

215 bottom The insignia of the prince-bishop, surrounded by allegorical sandstone statues, can be seen above the main entrance.

216 top June concerts have been held in the palace and park behind it since 1922 as part of the annual Festival dedicated to Mozart.

216-217 The garden side of one of the wings of the Residence is shown here. As Johann Philipp von Schönborn wanted to move from the uncomfortable, cold Marienberg as soon as possible, work on the new castle proceeded with all due haste: more than 100 workers labored continuously in the main building yards.

217 Like every princely residence of the period, the court gardens were extremely important. Inspired by French baroque gardens, they surround the palace with colorful flowerbeds dotted with oddly-shaped bushes. Statues of chubby putti and mythological figures created by the court sculptor Peter Wagner are scattered throughout the park.

218-219 The self-supporting vault, which is revealed only as one climbs the three flights of stairs, is totally decorated with world-famous frescoes by Tiepolo. The solidity of this masterpiece of static architecture was definitively tested during the bombardment of 1945, when most of the Residence was destroyed.

Two of Neumann's creations are visible as you enter the vestibule: the staircase and the ceiling, true miracles of static engineering. The ceiling 18 by 32 m, covers the entire area of the grand staircase without the support of a single pillar. Everyone was sure it would collapse before completion, and one of Neumann's rival architects declared that he would hang himself from the ceiling if it held up. Irritated, Neumann asked the bishop prince to test the structure by firing cannon salvoes under it. No test was ever performed, but during the bombardment of 1945, when most of the Residence was destroyed, the staircase and the ceiling survived. The ceiling is also famous for being the largest existing fresco in the world. It is the work of a genius of Italian painting, Gian Battista Tiepolo, who like many other Italian artists of the period was paid handsomely to bring the fashionable style of Italy to Germany. The artist, assisted by his two sons, took three years to complete the ceiling and the other frescoes in the Residence.

Another Italian artist, Antonio Bossi, is responsible for the incredible stucco work in the *Weisser Hall* (the White Hall). Already at the edge of madness, Bossi unleashed his imagination in original, unique forms before succumbing permanently to his psychosis. The whiteness of this hall provides a rest for the eyes before entering the explosion of colours and gilt in the Imperial Hall. Here Bossi's stucco details provide a framework for the strange optical effects that Tiepolo created in his frescoes. Neumann's triumphs continue in the Court Chapel as well, a burst of spiral-shaped columns, curving balconies and intersecting arches, also embellished by Tiepolo's paintings. The Residence's treasures do not lie only in its halls, but in its immense cellars as well, where some of the finest wines of Franconia are produced and aged.

The splendid Baroque Gardens, with the Residence providing the background, are a yearly summer setting for a series of concerts dedicated to Mozart, as well as a lively Wine Festival featuring wine produced in its cellars.

220 left The photo shows the Audience Room with its great tapestries. An extremely elegant majolica stove can be seen in the corner.

220 top right The Hall of Mirrors was totally destroyed during the Second

World War, but thanks to the painstaking work of highly specialized artists, it was totally restored.

220 bottom right The Green Room is entirely covered in exquisite lacquered rococo panels.

221 Antonio Bossi did the stucco work for the Residence Chapel, a burst of columns, arches and gilt. The paintings on the altar of this small, opulent baroque church are by Tiepolo.

222 and 222-223
The artistic partnership between Bossi and Tiepolo created an unusual freedom of expression in the Emperor's Room. The stucco artist has allowed frescoes to appear from behind the folds of a curtain, as if on a stage. On the edges, a leg, a head, or a cloud peeps out from the frame, blurring the distinction between two- and three-dimensionality. The frescoes on the sides of the walls and on the ceiling show various scenes, including (bottom left) the marriage of Frederick Barbarossa to Beatrice of Burgundy, and (in the picture at right) the bishop of Würzburg and the duke of Franconia discussing "good government."

GIO. BTTA. TIEPO

224-225 The Garden Room, which opens out on ground level, was a "buffer zone" used for serving refreshments or as a place for musicians. Bossi hid mirrors within his stucco work that shine with a magical, mysterious light in the glow of the candles. The frescoes by Johann Zick show the contrast between rigid court formality and utopian rustic abandon. The main painting (bottom left) shows the "Banquet of the Gods."

THE NEUE RESIDENCE OF BAMBERG

226 top left
The Neue Rezidenz
courtyard holds the
Rose Garden with
its bold sculptures
by Ferdinand Tietz.

226 top right
The west wing of the
palace is the work of
the Nuremberg
artist Jacob Wolff.
The two wings facing
the cathedral were
commissioned to

Leonard
Dientzenhofer by
the Elector Lothar
Franz von
Schönborn.
Neumann's plan for
the third wing could
not be completed due
to lack of funds
following the Second
Spanish War of
Succession.

226-227 The Rose
Garden is a burst

of splendid, brightly
colored, fragrant
flowers.

227 bottom left
Passion for the
Orient was great
during the baroque
period. Exotic themes
and decorations
recur in the
furnishings, such
as this large tapestry
depicting a Chinese
marriage.

Like Rome, Bamberg bears the architectural mark of the secular power of the Church. On the hill that dominates the city center, the same square holds two opposing examples of religious power: the cathedral, the house of God, with its solid and austere Gothic appearance and its four spires that seem to pierce the sky, represents the Church's power of guidance and salvation, while on the opposite side of the square, between the cathedral and the city, stands the sumptuous Residence, the home of the bishop, symbol of the vanity and temporal power of the clergy. The Renaissance-style west wing was completed between 1605 and 1611 by the city of Nuremberg's architect, Jakob Wolff the Elder, by order of the bishop prince Johann Philipp von Gebsattel. The two baroque wings facing the cathedral were commissioned by the man described as "one of the most gifted and impulsive princes who ever occupied the episcopal seat of Bamberg," the elector of Mainz, Lothar Franz von Schönborn (1693-1729). During the early years of his election, he had to restrain his mania for expanding and enriching his residence to meet the fashion of the time, because the cathedral Chapter had imposed a condition that formally forbade him from squandering finances in opulent buildings or improvements on already existing residences. When his insistent pressure finally resulted in a pontifical decree freeing him from this constraint, he immediately commissioned his architect, Leonhard Dientzenhofer, to design a new Residence, which in six years became the building we can admire today. Inside the Neue Residenz is the State Library, with an exceptional collection of 4500 manuscripts dating as far back as the 5th century, 3400 incunabula and 70,000 drawings. The guided visit leads through the Grand Halls, full of magnificent furniture, porcelains and carpets, and the Imperial Hall, a large room which in reality has a rather low ceiling, but which uses perspective frescoes with optical illusions – by the court painter Melchior Steidl – to give an impression of openness and space. Enclosed within the wings of the Residence is the *Rosegarten* (the Rose Garden), graced by the fragrance of a thousand varieties of roses, with bold statues by Ferdinand Tietz eternally overlooking the old roofs of the city below.

227 top right Finely
painted Oriental-style
decorations adorn the
wooden panels in the
Chinese Room in the
Neue Residence.

227 bottom right
The Imperial Hall
is the center of the
Grand Halls; it is
a large, rather low
room in which the
court painter Melchior
Steidl used perspective
frescoes to make the
ceiling appear higher.

THE BAYREUTH HERMITAGE

228 left One of the great attractions of the Hermitage is the garden, considered one of the most beautiful English gardens in Germany. The paths and colorful parterres are interrupted by extravagant fountains. There is also an artificial grotto and fake ruins, once used as a theater.

Bayreuth is a city with medieval roots, although the architecture of the Margravine Wilhelmine left its elegant baroque imprint. The city is world famous for its astounding *Markgräfliches Opernhaus* (the margravine's most beautiful gift to the city) and the Wagner Festival, and is scattered with splendid palaces and works of art, which make it one of the most attractive cities in northern Bavaria. The city center has two castles: the Renaissance-style *Altes Schloss* (16th-17th century) and the sumptuous *Neues Schloss*, which is also touched by the creative hand of the margravine's, but the most representative and romantic castle is located outside the city gates, among wheat fields and woodlands.

The Hermitage was built around the middle of the 18th century by the margravine Georg Wilhelm, as an ascetic refuge from his luxurious court, and was given to Wilhelmine by her husband Friederich, the successor to the throne of Bayreuth.

The Prussian princess was an emancipated, intelligent and energetic woman who was a talented painter, musician and writer. The daughter of Friederich Wilhelm I and favorite sister of Fredrick the Great, she could have become the future queen of England, but a mistaken political move by her father took her to Bayreuth, a provincial and colorless city in Franconia. Nevertheless, the young Wilhelmine was not to be outdone, and decided to transform Bayreuth

into a brilliant center for the arts, using the best artists and artisans of the time. The spartan Hermitage was transformed into a splendid summer residence, in which the margravine took refuge with her artist friends and penned her memories in emotional writings that became a brilliant piece of literature. The rococo palace became the background for the gardens on which the Margrave focused her creative attention. The gardens of the Hermitage were already famous in Bavaria for their design, which was *avant-garde* for the time.

Inspired by the theatrical effect produced by the position of the gardens, Wilhelmine made changes that satisfied her taste for the *mise-en-scène*. She brought in many statues and artificial ruins, among the most spectacular of which were the ruins of the theater. Wilhelmine herself and her friend Voltaire appeared on the stage in *Bajazet*, a tragedy by the French playwright Racine.

The *Neues Schloss* confirms the sensation that the buildings are almost a theatrical backdrop for the gardens.

In the center of the two curved side wings is the isolated *Sonnentempel* (the Sun Temple). Its extravagant covering of fragments of colored glass and blue and green rocks is absolutely unique. Complementing the dazzling effect are the golden Apollo statues on the cupola of the temple, with a team of four horses pulling the sun coach, symbol of absolute power in the style of Louis XIV of France

228 right The Sun Temple is on the Hermitage's formal side, from which the Orangerie extends in two semicircular wings. The outside walls of the complex are covered with fragments of pebbles and colored rocks, an unusual technique rarely used for exteriors.

228-229 The Hermitage's Old Castle was built by the Margrave Georg Wilhelm. The four-winged structure was then presented to the Margrave Wilhelmine, who added two side wings and transformed the interior.

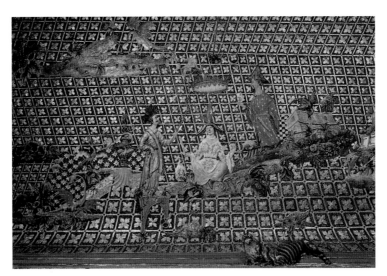

229 top The sumptuous yet intimate Japanese Room at the Hermitage has enamel relief work, some of which, the gift of Friederick the Great, comes from the Far East. Other enamel work was based on ideas by the Margravine Wilhelmine and completed with her assistance. This photo shows a detail of the ceiling with its unusual Oriental motifs.

230 top left The original furnishings still stand in the Gothic-style chapel. The altar by Junker, is one of the most precious pictorial works of the period.

230 top right The Bed Chamber is in true neoclassical style, decorated with panelling and a pink silk canopy embroidered with pure gold thread.

JOHANNISBURG CASTLE IN ASCHAFFENBURG

The city of Aschaffenburg stands on the Main River in Spessart, the far western corner of Bavaria.

In contrast to the gentle natural landscape, the city is a row of massive stone façades along the river, the most imposing of which is Schloss Johannisburg, a legacy of the immense secular power wielded by the prince-bishops of Mainz, who reigned from the 10th to the early 19th centuries. Before being appointed arch prince-bishops and elector of Mainz, Johann Schweikhard von Kronberg had to swear to restore the ruins of the castle of Aschaffenburg, which had been destroyed by the Margrave of Kulmbach. The Renaissance palace, the archbishop's second residence, was built between 1604 and 1614 on a design by Georg Riedinger. A child of his time, the elector yearned for a *grandeur* that would befit his position as an elector of the Holy Roman Empire.

He thus created an imposing red sandstone palace, consisting of four wings with a massive tower at each corner, spending the equivalent of forty-five million marks.

The Johannisburg is one of the most important works of the German Renaissance, as well as one of the largest castles in Germany built at one time based on a single design, and is a grandiose introduction to the architecture of state castles typical of the modern era.

230-231 A witness to the immense secular power of the prince-bishops of Mainz, who ruled here from the 10th to the 19th centuries, Johannisburg Castle's imposing façade is reflected in the Main River.

231 top Titus' Arch is depicted in one of the pieces in the collection of little cork models on display at Johannisburg Castle.

231 bottom The interior of the magnificent residence is furnished in Neoclassical style, with interesting furniture from the late 18th century.

SCHLOSS *EHRENBURG*

232 top left
The picture is a view of one of the two side pavilions, with the façade adorned by architectural balconies.

232 top right *The main entrance to Ehrenburg opens to form the Court of Honour on the broad square. The three segments that make it up date back to*

the late 17th-century baroque structure, but the façade was redone in neo-Gothic English style in the early 19th century.

232-233
The marvelous Party Room, which dates back to the time of Duke Albrecht, is almost entirely covered with extraordinary stucco

decorations by Carlo Domenico and Bartolomeo Lucchese. It is known as the Hall of Giants due to the twenty-eight massive male caryatid figures who appear to hold up the ceiling. Each one holds a candelabra in an outstretched arm, with the other arm bent above his head to support the ceiling.

*C*oburg is the capital of Coburgerland, located among the hills of upper Franconia and the last remnants of the Thuringian Forest. Its beautiful historic downtown area still exudes that aristocratic elegance that characterized it until the last century. On the broad Schlossplatz, where fine summer concerts are held among the splendid flowerbeds, is Schloss Ehrenburg, the ducal palace and residence of the Saxe-Coburg-Gotha family until 1920. The powerful family was allied with royal families all over Europe. Albert, the beloved prince consort of Queen Victoria of England, whose descendants still hold the British throne, was descended from this family. Queen Victoria herself, who was a frequent guest at Ehrenburg, was responsible for introducing something which was at the time an absolute luxury and novelty, and which now, among the astonishing riches of the residence, is one of the most popular curiosities for visitors: Germany's first flush toilet, a convenience to which the queen had become accustomed in England and which she was absolutely unwilling to do without during her long stays at Coburg.

Ehrenburg has a neo-Gothic appearance, primarily due to the final retouches of 1811, but the original edifice was built in 1543 by order of Duke Johann Ernst, on the site of a thirteenth-century convent. At that time he was one of the first rulers north of the Alps to abandon a safer but undeniably more austere fortified dwelling on a hill for a more comfortable, stately residence in the center of the city. After the Thirty Years' War, during which Coburg was invaded by enemy troops, the castle was abandoned for nearly a half a century. Duke Albrecht occupied it in 1680 and restored and remodeled it according to the baroque tastes of the times. He is responsible for the opulent Hall of Giants, which owes its artistic importance to its masterpiece of stucco decoration. Neoclassicism left a clear mark on Ehrenburg; many rooms were remodeled under Duke Ernst I (1806-1844), and most of the rococo and baroque furniture was replaced by furnishings, bronzes and clocks bought especially in Paris.

The furnishings in the rooms have been left almost completely as they were, including the family photographs of Queen Victoria on the tables, and this is one of the castle's major attractions. In its less stately and more residential rooms, the place almost seems still inhabited, offering a rare glimpse into a usually inaccessible world.

233 The portraits of Coburg nobles in the Family Room include a portrait of Prince Albert, who married his cousin Victoria, the British monarch. Devastated by the death of her beloved husband at only 42 years old, the queen (who ruled for 54 years) mourned him until her death.

FORTIFIED CASTLES, MEDIEVAL SPLENDORS

234 top In 1277 Pottenstein Castle, located on a steep cliff of dolomitic rock, provided refuge for Saint Elizabeth, who had fled Thuringia after the death of her husband. By the 18th century the castle had fallen into ruins: a Nuremberg pharmacist finally put a halt to its destruction in 1878 when he rebuilt several parts of the castle.

Bavaria's position in the heart of Europe has made it a territory of transit, sometimes for purposes of trade, but more often for conquest.

Ever since ancient times, primitive fortresses of wood and earth were erected to defend the population. When the Romans conquered the ancient territory of Bavaria, they often built their rock fortresses on the ruins of primitive fortifications which they themselves had vanquished.

As the centuries passed, the realm of Bavaria expanded and became richer and more enticing to the peoples on its borders. The Bavarians themselves felt an increasing sense of independence and a desire for conquest.

All over Europe trade was beginning to flourish, and important trading routes, such as the Salt Road and the Iron Road, were opening up and traversing its borders. Numerous fortresses sprang up to protect cities, rivers and valleys and defend these merchant routes. This type of defensive architecture reached its zenith during the medieval Age of Chivalry.

In mountainous areas, the fortresses are perched on rocky heights in impossible positions, and almost seem sculpted in the rock.

Their position alone was sufficient to dissuade the most hardened assailant. Fortified castles in hilly areas are true fortified citadels, often with various circular fortifications, and from a distance look like giant transatlantic liners floating in a green see.

On the plains, in addition to massive walls, the only other defense possible was to surround the castle with water, using the natural attributes of the countryside. Thus, many of the towers and bastions that we still find so romantic today are reflected in lakes, rivers, ponds and wide moats. Wherever they are built, and however diverse their appearances, their structures, all designed for defense, have much in common, including walls, turrets and slit windows to protect their defenders, massive gates with drawbridges, watchtowers, guard towers with alarm bells, wells and granaries to resist sieges, and the residential portion for the noble and his court, a bit more comfortable than the other wings but still very austere and cramped.

The lack of space was another common denominator for these fortresses, which during times of war became refuges for a majority of the population. By the end of the Middle Ages, changing techniques of war made these structures obsolete, and in pursuit of a new-found taste for comfort and luxury, the nobles abandoned them. Many fell into ruin, but many were recovered and restored: the largest have been converted into museums with art galleries open to the public, and the smaller ones were purchased by private parties who restored them not only as residences, but also as lovely inns, comfortable restaurants or small private museums.

234 bottom A visit to the medieval castle of Rosenburg, near Riedenburg on eastern Bavaria's border with Franconia, is a true trip back into the past. In its courtyard, trainers in period costumes and their birds of prey provide visitors with an extraordinary demonstration of hunting with these majestic birds, taking observers back into the past as they watch these raptors gliding over the beautiful Altmühl Valley.

234-235 The tall, slender tower of Veldenstein fortress is the emblem of Neuhaus an der Pegnitz, an ancient village with red-tiled roofs and typical lattice-work houses. In 1007 this important commercial city on the southern edge of the dense Veldenstein forest was conquered by Henry II for his new Bamberg diocese.

235 top
The Niederhaus fortress is connected to the Oberhaus fortress above by a long rounds walk which has a splendid view of the city, with the colorful confluence of the three rivers that surround it: the pale Danube, the muddy Inn and the deep green Ilz.

236-237 The town of Füssen has an imposing castle with turreted walls and portals known as Hohes Schloss, which dates back to a 4th-century Roman fort. The fortress was built in 1219 and underwent many changes over the centuries, but the transformation into a castle did not alter its defensive character.

238-239 The village of Burghausen with its elegant architecture characteristic of the Inn-Salzach region stands on the banks of the Salzach River under the protective gaze of its massive fortress, which guarded the city's profitable salt trade for over 300 years.

238 top In order to strengthen the defensive power of the fortress, the six courtyards were independent and fortified, separated by deep moats that permitted troops and inhabitants to resist assaults and sieges for long periods of time.

THE BURGHAUSEN FORTRESS

"There is the underground city!" cried Napoleon as he crossed the Salzach River with his troops. It was an appropriate comment, reflecting the defensive position of the city in its role as an important military post along the Austrian-Bavarian border. Featuring the colorful architecture typical of the Inn-Salzach area, this lovely city unwinds along the Salzach River, its main street in the shadow of the longest fortress in Europe, a true citadel of 1030 m.

There are no longer any traces of the old castle from the year 1090, but the foundation walls, the cellars of Duke Henry XII and the inner chapel dating from the 13th century can still be admired in the main courtyard.

In the late fifteenth century, the continuous threat of the Turks prompted an expansion of the fortress that went on for more than ten years; today, most of its structures date from 1480 to 1490. In medieval times, each of the six courtyards that comprise it were separated by a moat, a drawbridge and a gate. To the north, the tuff rise on which the fortress was built expands to 100 m wide, becoming a low terrace. This was the most vulnerable part of the fortress, and indeed, its largest edifice, which enclosed the sixth courtyard to the north and was used as a granary and barracks, was demolished by Napoleon so that it could never again be used as a defense against him. Shortly thereafter, most of the structures which stood around what is now a large green square, were sold to private parties. This was the fate of almost all the buildings, which are still occupied by private owners. Although the current owners do not permit their homes to be visited, as you pass from courtyard to courtyard among the still-inhabited buildings within the castle walls, there is an evocative impression that the fortress is still alive, as it was in the past, when the buildings that now are home to the tranquil citizens of Burghausen served as quarters for soldiers, servants, court officials and their families. In the sixth courtyard the names of the buildings still echo the functions of the people that inhabited them: to the west, built in the 14th century, are the guest quarters and those of the chancellor and the beneficiaries. The round towers to the east and that of the income registrar, carpenters and chimney sweeps, date back to the 15th century, when the buildings, the craftsmen's workshops and a stable completed the courtyard. Crossing a bridge, which is no longer the original, you come to the fifth courtyard. To the east is the building that housed the tax office, and behind it is the courtyard's main point of interest, the outer chapel. This Gothic gem was built by the royal couple that is still commemorated every four years at Landshut, in a famous historical reconstruction of their wedding – Georg the Rich, the Duke of Landshut, and Jadwiga, the daughter of the king of Poland.

239 top The chapel is the point of attraction in the fifth courtyard. A jewel of Gothic style with its pointed bell tower, it was donated to the castle by Duke George the Rich and Jadwiga, the daughter of the King of Poland.

239 bottom The early 16th century clock tower with its added kiosk stands in the center of the broad green open space in the sixth courtyard.

240 left This wooden statue of St. Martin stands in the inner chapel of the main courtyard.

240 right The Ducal Hall in the first courtyard holds two museums. The Civic Museum contains terra-cotta items, antique furniture, weapons, uniforms and folk

costumes, while the State Museum displays paintings and tapestries form the national Bavarian collection. The photo shows an ornamental relief of the castle.

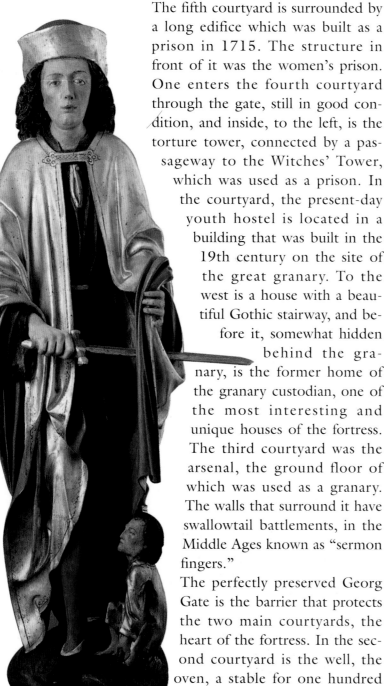

The fifth courtyard is surrounded by a long edifice which was built as a prison in 1715. The structure in front of it was the women's prison. One enters the fourth courtyard through the gate, still in good condition, and inside, to the left, is the torture tower, connected by a passageway to the Witches' Tower, which was used as a prison. In the courtyard, the present-day youth hostel is located in a building that was built in the 19th century on the site of the great granary. To the west is a house with a beautiful Gothic stairway, and before it, somewhat hidden behind the granary, is the former home of the granary custodian, one of the most interesting and unique houses of the fortress. The third courtyard was the arsenal, the ground floor of which was used as a granary. The walls that surround it have swallowtail battlements, in the Middle Ages known as "sermon fingers."

The perfectly preserved Georg Gate is the barrier that protects the two main courtyards, the heart of the fortress. In the second courtyard is the well, the oven, a stable for one hundred horses and the servants' and grooms' quarters. Access to the first courtyard is over a moat 8 m deep and 28 m wide and two gates. The various parts of the residential castle, which now holds the State Museum and the Municipal Museum, open up around the courtyard, but for centuries the walls served as a defense and sometimes as a prison for the lords of the time. Even the unfortunate Jadwiga, principal of the famous "Landshut Marriage", pageant that commemorates her wedding, ended her days there after many years of confinement. The official reason for her imprisonment was that she had borne her husband no male heirs, but the reports of the time maintained that she, ignored by an increasingly absent and unfaithful husband, was caught seeking solace with the fortress' cook.

240-241 This photo shows a view of the complex's oldest buildings, which date back to the Gothic period. In the 1st century BC there was a Celtic fortress on the southernmost point of the ridge (the current position of the residential palace). The fortress took on its present form over the centuries, but the inner chapel and the castle cellars from 1200 can still be admired in their original form.

241 bottom
The stairway on the left wing of the first courtyard, Dürnitz, leads to a Renaissance Gothic room with round arches, which served as a meeting and ball room. The ballroom for servants and domestics was on the first floor.

HARBURG CASTLE

Near the famous Romantic Road in the northwestern part of Bavarian Allgäu-Swabia, this castle, which seems to come from a fable of dragons and knights, dominates the lovely town with its lattice-work houses. Its towers and turrets rising out of the green woods that surround it make it easy to imagine that its impregnable walls are protecting the long slumber of Sleeping Beauty. First mentioned in an official document in 1093, this fortress was built to defend the imperial road from Nördlingen to Donauwörth. In 1295 the castle was given to the faithful Counts – later Princes – of Oettingen, a privilege which became hereditary in 1407 (their descendants still own it). Today the castle, an architectural hodgepodge that spans seven centuries, is one of the best preserved complexes of its type in southern Germany. The main courtyard can be reached through a series of medieval defensive structures and is surrounded by several interesting functional structures, such as the *Kastenhaus*, the old granary and the *Burgtvogtei*, the 16th-century manor house, now transformed into a small, picturesque hotel-restaurant. The oldest part still standing, the *Diebsturm*, or Thieves' Tower, dates back to the 12th century. The *Fürstenbau*, a 16th-century structure, houses the priceless collection of art that the lords of the castle collected over the centuries, including some masterpieces in wood by the inimitable Tilman Riemenschneider.

WILLIBALDSBURG FORTRESS

244 The fortress holds the Jura Museum. This splendid Jurassic museum gives an evocative picture of prehistoric life in this part of Bavaria. It has a large collection of fossils found nearby, including enormous fish (top), and a rare, intact example of Archaeopteryx (bottom), the link between reptiles and birds.

244-245 The defensive and war-like aspects of the Willibaldsburg fortress made it an impregnable bulwark protecting the baroque city of Eichstätt below and the important Altmühl River and commercial route. At its peak, the fortress was one of the most sumptuous castles in Germany.

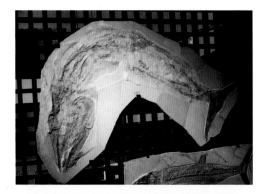

The city of Eichstädt is a small baroque jewel located in the heart of the natural park of the Altmühltal, a valley traversed by the Altmühl River, full of breathtaking scenery and priceless architectural treasures. Above the city stands one of the most important fortified castles in the entire valley. Built on a steep slope for defensive purposes, the large complex with its angular towers was built by order of Bishop Berthold von Eichstätt in 1393 and remained a bishop's residence until 1780. In 1609, the famous architect Elias Holl, who designed the Augsburg City Hall, was hired to build the imposing *Gemmingenbau*. The residential palace now holds the Jura-Museum, with one of the most interesting fossil collections in Bavaria, including unique, extremely rare examples of *Archaeopteryx* found in the area. Willibaldsburg was once one of the most sumptuous castles in Germany. After the Thirty Years' War it was further fortified and transformed into a citadel. Like most fortified residences, with the advent of more peaceful times and government well-being, the bishop princes of Eichstätt decided to build a sumptuous palace in the city, thus giving it the prestigious Residence with its remarkable rococo and neoclassical rooms.

245 top *Magnificent Willibaldsburg emerges in the distance against the placid landscape of the Altmühl Valley.*

The English missionary monk Willibald founded Eichstätt in 745 and became its first bishop.

PRUNN CASTLE

246 top left The simple little chapel is embellished by stucco work on the ceiling and a graceful wooden altar.

246 top right The interior of the fortress is quite bare, due in part to the fact that one of its last uses was as a Franciscan monastery but the decorations around the doors are worthy of interest and the windows offer a bird's-eye view of the valley and the river.

246-247 Looking like a continuation of the rock on which they were built, the walls of the Prunn fortress hid the first manuscript of the Legend of the Nibelungen for two centuries. The manuscript was discovered accidentally during remodeling work in 1575.

The castle can be seen in the distance from the valley.

In seeming defiance of human reason, it was constructed on a rock 70 m high overlooking the Altmühl River, and appears to be practically suspended from it.

It is impossible not to marvel at how, almost a thousand years ago, such solid and beautiful buildings capable of resisting wartime attacks and the ravages of time could be built in such seemingly impossible positions. While its view from the bottom of the valley is certainly beautiful, the panorama visible from the castle's rooms and walls is truly breathtaking, with a bird's eye view of the Altmühl valley. It runs uninterrupted for miles and miles, following the tranquil course of the river, which curls through the deep green pine woods, the golden yellow rape fields and the white villages dotted with red. Period documents show that the castle was already in existence in 1037. Its long history has seen many lords, including the von Prunn family, who gave it its name, the Dukes of Bavaria, the brotherhood of the Jesuits of Ingolstadt, and finally, in 1803, the State of Bavaria. The castle is famous for its *Prunn Codex*, an antique manuscript from around 1300, which was accidentally found during a Renaissance restoration of its interior.

The manuscript recounts the first "Song of the Nibelungen," which inspired Wagner to write his Ring cycle.

247 top Since 1037, when the fortress on the promontory was first mentioned, many lords have contended for its possession, including the von Prunn nobles, who gave it its name.

247 bottom The beautiful fortified structure stands precariously on a 230-ft (70-m) cliff. In ancient times it was the most formidable fortress in the Altmühl Valley.

THE FORTRESS OF NUREMBERG

Nuremberg is the second largest city in Bavaria and the capital of one of its regions, Franconia. Because of its key position on many important trading routes, the city reached its economic apex in the Middle Ages, and in 1356, in an edict known as the "Golden Bull," the Emperor Charles IV ruled that each newly elected German king had to hold his first Diet at Nuremberg. With the discovery of America, the economic power of the city declined, but in the 17th century Nuremberg was equally famous for its paintings and its sculptures. Its nearly legendary status in the eyes of many Germans continued over time, so that even Hitler chose it as the seat of his government and the future capital of his empire. After the war, the Allies also recognized its symbolic importance and chose it as the seat for the famous Nuremberg trials of surviving Nazi leaders.

The *Burg* (fortress), perched on a rock at the edge of the old city, gives Nuremberg its unmistakable profile. The odd-looking group of buildings that make it up has grown over the centuries and actually consists of two castles joined together. On the eastern tip of the rocky spur is *Burggrafenburg* (the Count's Fortress), which came into the possession of the Zoller family in the 12th century. This powerful family was at variance with the Imperial City of Nuremberg, which held Kaiserburg, the other fortress on the rock. The conflict went on interminably, and the harshest affront to Count Zoller occurred when the citizens built a new fortified tower right in front of his fortress. The tower, completed in only five months while the Count was away travelling, was used to spy on Burggrafenburg. In 1427 the Zoller family lost interest in the old ruin and sold it to the city. *Kaiserburg* (the Imperial Fortress), located on the western tip of the promontory, is the most impressive part of the complex. The first fortress was built in 1050 by King Henry III; around the middle of the 12th century Emperor Conrad III built *Kaiserburg*, which was then expanded and transformed into an imperial residence by

248-249 The city of Nuremberg is first mentioned as "Nuremberc" in an imperial document of 1050. In 1219 it was granted the status of a free imperial city, which it maintained until 1806. Many Imperial Diets were held here, and it was also the seat of the Imperial Court.

249 top A 1492 illustration shows the city surrounded by walls (almost all of which still remain) and dominated by the fortress. The tall towers of the churches of St. Sebald and St. Lawrence can be seen below it; even today they are important artistic monuments in the city.

250 *The double Romanesque chapel from the 12th century is architecturally the most important part of the fortress. The large sandstone columns of the lower chapel stand in sharp contrast to the slender columns in the Emperor's Chapel, with vaults which almost seem weightless.*

Frederick I Barbarossa around 1200. The German empire had no capital, and its emperors and their entourages moved from one residence to another. It is easy to imagine the importance of the fortress of Nuremberg if you consider that from 1050 to 1571 all emperors stayed there, although none of them for long periods of time. This explains the fact that inside the fortress everything appears quite bare and stripped of furnishings. This is not due to the fires and wars the fortress suffered, but

was how it looked when the Emperor and his court were not there. Indeed, the shrewd, thrifty citizens of Nuremberg loaned their finest furniture and furnishings to the fortress when the Emperor announced a visit. After he left, the owners took everything back home.

The inner courtyard of *Kaiserburg* is enclosed within a long Gothic-style *Palas* with the residential and state rooms of the emperor and his court. Inside is a lovely two-story chapel, with the upper floor reserved to the nobility and the lower to the servants. In the center of the courtyard outside *Kaiserburg*, dominated by the massive Sinwell Tower, is the house that contains the *Tiefer Brunnen* (Deep Well), fully 50 m deep, which provided water to the fortress as early as the 12th century.

In 1427 the western tip of the promontory was also taken by the city and incorporated into its defenses, but it remained the property of the Holy Roman Empire.

The oldest part of the fortress is the *Fünfeckturm* (Pentagonal Tower), the only remaining part of the original fortress, which shares the eastern part of the promontory with the massive Luginslandturm. After the Zoller family was driven out, the citizens connected the two towers with the Gothic *Kaiserstallung* (the Imperial Stables), which was then used as a granary and now serves as a youth hostel.

250-251 This is a view of the Tiergärtnertor Platz at the foot of the Kaiserburg Residential Palace. The home of Albrecht Dürer, now a museum, stands on the square.

251 top The photo shows Kaiserburg's outer court with the Well House in the center. The Deep Well was dug into the rock to a depth of 50 m. Two truss structures from the 15th and 16th centuries stand in the southwest corner. The lower part of imposing Sinwell Tower dates back to the 12th century, while the upper portion is from 1560.

THE MARIENBERG FORTRESS

The fortress stands on a hill that dominates the city of Würzburg and the Main River, on the same site where the Celts built their fortifications around 1000 BC. The *Marienkirche* (which can be seen within the fortress), one of the oldest churches in Germany, was built in the 8th century, and in the 13th century the construction and fortification of the Marienberg citadel began. From 1253 to 1720 it served as the residence of the prince-bishops. The castle was transformed into a citadel through various important construction works, which were completed by bishop Rudolf von Scherenberg (1466-1495). Its present-day appearance is the work of Bishop Julius Echter von Mespelbrunn (1573-1617). The Mainfrankisches Museum, Franconia's art museum, is located in the Arsenal. It holds a superb collection of wooden sculptures by one of Germany's greatest sculptors of wood, Tilman Riemenschneider. Riemenschneider lived in Würzburg from 1483 to 1531, when he was killed in a bloody battle during the Peasants' Revolt. At the entrance to the museum is an interesting portrait gallery with portraits of the electors of Würzburg, including the man responsible for building the Residence, Johann Philipp von Schönborn.

252 top
The surrounding moat has been transformed into pleasant gardens where summer shows are held. In the background, one can glimpse the baroque, onion-shaped cupola of the Kiliani Tower, built when the castle was being fortified in the 13th century.

252 centre The Main and Franconia Museum located in the former arsenal and bastion of Echter offers a representative look at 2000 years of regional history. Its works are significant and varied, including items such as swords and weapons from this arsenal, famous paintings by local artists and forest rangers, sculptures by Tilman Riemenschneider, handicrafts and everyday objects and old folk costumes.

252 bottom The great winepresses in the arsenal's old section tell the story of wine-growing in the area.

252-253 Resting on a hill covered with vineyards, the Marienberg fortress, an important work of defensive architecture, dominates the city of Würzburg and the Main River.

253 top
The Romanesque *Marienkirche* is the oldest monument in Marienberg. It was built on the hill in the 7th century as a sign of devotion to the Virgin Mary, and the fortress was later built around it.

254 top left
This photo clearly shows the defensive power of the fortress. One of the two circles of walls with its massive guard towers can be seen below the Veste Coburg's high, sheer walls.

254 top right
The Veste Coburg is one of the largest fortresses in Germany. Its imposing 200x80 m oval form gave it the name of Fränkische Krone, the Crown of Franconia.

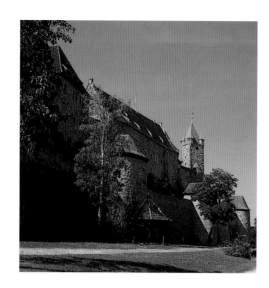

VESTE COBURG

254-255 *One enters from the east side over an 18th-century bridge through a baroque portal from 1671. The door to the back, which leads to the first circle of walls, is surmounted by a tower built in 1911 by the czar Ferdinand of Bulgaria, from the house of Coburg-Gotha.*

255 *top*
The Fürstenbau, *the princely palace built in the 16th century, faces the inner courtyard. Today's façade is the result of remodelling in the lattice-work style of Franconia.*

255 bottom *The thick barrier of the second wall is the last defensive bastion and completely surrounds the inner courtyards, where there are various residential and utility buildings.*

One of the most beautiful fortresses in Europe, Veste Coburg stands on the top of a hill occupied by the Ehrenburg, the city palace park, which reaches the outermost of its three circular fortifications.

From a distance, the numerous watchtowers and the gabled roofs rise from the bands of walls like the points of a crown, giving this fortress its Bavarian name of *Fränkische Krone*, or the Crown of Franconia. The city of Coburg, located in the far north of Franconia, was under the jurisdiction of the Dukes of Saxe-Coburg-Gotha until 1920, when the citizens voted to join Upper Franconia, thus becoming Bavarian. The fortress boasts 750 years of history. In 1353 it belonged to the Wettin family, the rulers of Saxony and Thuringia, and in the 16th century it became one of their main residences.

The descendants of the Wettin family, the Dukes of Coburg, used it as a residence until 1918. The Gothic-style oldest portion was built between the 14th and 16th centuries, when the first circle of fortifications was constructed.

During the 16th century the fortress was transformed into a citadel, and Lucas Cranach the Elder, who stayed there often, helped transform it into a princely residence.

The outer bastions were added during the following two centuries.

The *Steinerne Kemenate*, which holds a rich collection of art, with works by Cranach, Dürer, Schongauer and Rembrandt, is located to the left of the beautiful courtyard.

In the Hunting Room, the 1632 wall covering, with rare inlay work and carvings, is one of the most beautiful works of its kind.

In 1530 Martin Luther took refuge within its walls, where he paced the silent gardens and rooms as the Diet of Augsburg deliberated its verdict in his heresy trial. The great reformer's room in the fortress can still be visited today.

256 This photo shows one of his paintings at the Veste Coburg, a portrait of Johann der Beständige, the bishop prince of Saxony.

256-257 The interior of the Prince's Palace is richly furnished with Renaissance and baroque furniture.

257 top One of the most important rooms in the fortress is the Luther Room, named after Martin Luther, who stayed at the Veste Coburg in 1530. A famous portrait of the reformer by Lucas Cranach the Elder hangs on one of the walls.

257 center A collection of coaches and sleds is on display on the ground floor of the Herzoginbau. Of special note are the wedding coaches from the 16th century and the tournament sleds from the 17th to the 18th centuries.

257 bottom A lavish collection of weapons and war apparatus can be seen in the Guard Room.

Castles of the Loire

INTRODUCTION

From Giens to Angers, by the calm waters of what has been called the loveliest river in France and along its major tributaries, hundreds of fortresses and castles appear as if by magic from the woods. But why should there be so many princely residences in this area?

One tragic night 600 years ago, the Burgundians put Paris to fire and sword. Tanguy du Châtel, a faithful servant of King Charles VI, hastened to the palace and, with a group of horsemen, escorted the 15-year-old dauphin of France to safety at Chinon Castle. Thus, on the night of May 28, 1418, began the history of the castles of the Loire. For a century the court of the kings of France, with their

260 top The walls of Chaumont Castle, shrouded in the morning mist, conceal a multitude of secrets and mysteries.

260-261 Chambord Castle, so grandiose as to seem almost unreal, looms up in the distance like a mirage.

261 Shooting parties take place every year in the huge grounds of Cheverny Castle, and the pack of dogs are exercised along the paths of the park under the guidance of a trainer every day.

retinue of noblemen and dignitaries, moved to the banks of the river. The dauphin (who ascended to the throne as Charles VII) and his successors found the Loire Valley to be the ideal refuge from the threats of a turbulent, unsafe capital. Great castles were built, ancient city walls restored and patrician residences erected, housing a wealth of splendors, intrigues, vendettas, courtly pageants and decadent love affairs.

But in a letter written on his return from Madrid on March 15, 1528, Francis I manifested the desire to return "to sojourn in the good city of Paris." The Loire had lost the privilege of being the Valley of Kings. When the court left, the noblemen who had built princely residences, no less magnificent than the royal castles, left too. Thus the lights went out on that enchanted world that, centuries later, still evokes a dreamlike fascination. Princes and kings, courtiers and minstrels, queens and dukes still seem to tread that great stage. An invisible hand holds the strings of their memories. From the time of Louis XI to the present day, it has been said, the centuries have never obscured the fame of this garden, where François Rabelais plucked the roses of life. A million tourists visit it every year not only because of the castles, but also for the countryside, the cuisine, and the secrets held by a region that always has something to say. The villages, with their quiet squares basking in the sun, encircle the larger towns, where the living heart of the Loire beats. Through its markets, riverside restaurants and souvenir shops, to the backdrops of its better known castles, the history of the Loire is recounted in "sound and light." Every stone tells a story, every garden bears witness to the idle pleasures of a king, and every drawing room rings with the echoes of a bygone world. But the Loire Valley is only the main artery of a much larger green heart, also studded with castles steeped in history; the whole region is just waiting to be discovered, by traveling from castle to castle like a courtly minstrel. There are the more famous ones, perched on its banks or nestled in the woods: Chambord, Chenonceau, Blois, Amboise, Azay-le-Rideau, Langeais, Chinon, and so on. To the south, in the ancient land of Berry, there are the more defensive castles designed as military outposts, like the fortress of Culan, Meillant Castle, shrouded in the green mantle of the forest of the same name, and the castle of Ainay-le-Vieil. And there are the lesser known castles to the north, behind the Loire, such as Châteaudun, perched on a steep crag, Montigny-le-Gannelon, with its magnificent furnishings, Maintenon, still as it was when Louis XIV's secret wife lived there and, just outside Paris, Anet Castle, the little kingdom of Diane de Poitiers, mistress of King Henry II, which brings to an end the romantic and dissolute history of the Loire Valley castles.

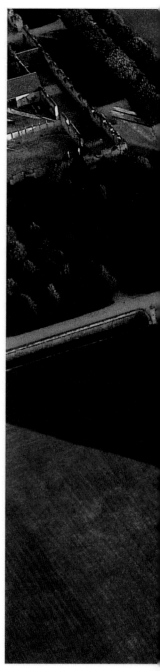

266-267 The village of Chenonceaux, about 19 miles from Tours, is famous for the castle of almost the same name (Chenonceau without the "x"), built in the early 16th century for Thomas Bohier, tax collector under Charles VIII, Louis XII and Francis I.

268-269 The castle of Sully-sur-Loire, which has the tallest slate roof in the Loire Valley, stands like an island of pale stone suspended over the water.

The castle of Sully-sur-Loire

Chambord Castle

Valençay Castle

Ussé Castle

Azay-le-Rideau Castle

Amboise Castle

Anet

Collines
du Perche

Maintenon

Eure   Chartres

Châteaudun   Montargis

Montigny-le-Gannelon   Orléans

                              Loire

Talcy   Sully

                                        Gien

Chambord
Blois   La Verrerie
Chaumont   Beauregard
Tours   Cheverny
            Amboise
Langeais   La Chapelle D'Angillon
    Villandry   Chenonceaux   Cher
Ussé   Maupas
Saumur   Bourges
    Azay-le-Rideau
Chinon   Valençay

            Loches   Monts du Morvan

                        Bouges

                Indre

Azay-le-Ferron
                                    Meillant
                    Châteauroux

            Argenton   La Chatre   Ainay-le-Vieil

Angers

Loir

THE GENTLE SOUTHERN COUNTRYSIDE

At the southernmost border of the central Val de Loire region, before the architectural grandeur of the famous valley begins, the department of Cher has constructed the historical Jacques Coeur route, which leads to villages and castles. These castles were the theater of war centuries ago, when the area, which forms part of the ancient region once called Berry, divided the possessions of the king of France from those of the king of England. Visitors can still admire these outposts of bygone deeds, long roads and unusual itineraries entwining with the great river, until reaching Bouges Castle – with its precious furnishings – and Valençay Castle – residence of statesman Talleyrand – bring them back to the charm of castles that have never known war. In Culan, the 12th-century stronghold standing high on a spur of rock has the austere features of one who has known the hardships of sieges. It is an awe-inspiring fortress, with mighty round towers overlooking the Arnon. The great 15th-century fireplaces, two precious paintings attributed to Caravaggio, the original windows and precious historical relics testify to its past splendors. Its grandeur was due to the feats of Louis de Culan, admiral of France, who fought all over the world and was Joan of Arc's comrade in arms at Patay and Orléans. Famous personalities and leading statesmen have stayed at the grandiose castle, last but not least being General de Gaulle in November 1951. Indre, which borders on Cher, is another department whose treasures are worth a visit. The most romantic is the magnificent country home of George Sand at Nohant, an aristocratic mansion with many rooms and a peaceful garden on the outskirts of La Châtre village, which inspired the scenario often described in her novels. George Sand, born in Paris in the early 19th century, came to live at her grandmother's house as a child. From Chateauroux it's just a short trip to La Brenne, a little-known region that few tourists visit, except for the elite band of nature lovers who travel with sleeping bags and sleep under the stars. There are no trees, just scrub, moors, meadows, great silences and 400 ponds in this nook where unspoiled nature has an austere, melancholic charm. Every so often, scattered over the wide open spaces, there's a cottage, a castle, like the splendid castle of Azay-le-Ferron, or a secluded village. To the north of La Brenne are Bouges Castle and Valençay Castle, still in the gentle Berry countryside. Fields and forests lead to the discreet elegance of Bouges Castle, a severe square of pale Touraine stone with a classic beauty, devoid of pinnacles, in perfect Louis XV style. It recalls the Trianon at Versailles, partly because of the antique furnishings, collected in a lifetime's research by the last owners, M. and Mme. Viguier, who bought it in 1917.

271

GRACE AND STRENGTH: AINAY-LE-VIEIL CASTLE

Ainay-le-Vieil is the southernmost castle in the Loire Valley. The thick octagonal walls of this intact medieval fortress surround the Renaissance grace of the central building, added centuries later, next to the 16th-century Renaissance tower. It is still inhabited by the descendants of Charles de Chevenon de Bigny, the noble knight who bought the property from the Lord of Culan in 1467. It houses historical relics associated with Colbert, Marie Antoinette and, still longer ago, Louis XII and Anne of Brittany. The parapets pass from tower to tower, surrounding the castle with a continuous circle of walls that has won the impressive building the nickname of "Petit Carcassonne." In the great hall is a huge fireplace, meticulously carved with symbols and the royal initials L and A against a blue background of gilded fleurs-de-lys. When spring comes, a thousand varieties of old roses bloom in the castle garden, while in summer the historic castle presents thematic exhibitions and some very popular events.

272-273
Ainay-le-Vieil, the southernmost castle in the Loire Valley, on the borders of Berry, is an extraordinary medieval fortress dating from the 14th century. Massive towers intersect the polygonal design of the outer walls, which enclose the attractive inner courtyard of the castle, with its Renaissance tower and beautifully furnished interior. The castle has belonged for five centuries to the descendants of Charles de Chevenon de Bigny, the noble knight who bought the property from the Lord of Culan in 1467.

THE RESIDENCE OF BEAUTIFUL DUCHESS: VALENÇAY CASTLE

274 top and 274-275 Standing at the end of an avenue of plane trees, beyond a monumental gateway, Valençay Castle features classical lines intersected by the great central Renaissance- style keep. Much altered over the centuries, it was transformed by Talleyrand de Périgord into a magnificent gentleman's residence.

A few miles away, Valençay Castle bears witness to the splendors of the First Empire. "Lord of Talleyrand, it is my wish that you purchase a beautiful residence where you can receive the diplomatic corps and foreigners accredited to Paris," said Napoleon to his prime minister in 1803. Talleyrand did not need to be asked twice. At Valençay he found a ruined 16th-century castle, built by Jacques d'Estampes, with an east wing added in the 17th century. He transformed it into that perfection of style and furnishing that can still be admired today by moving from room to room along the grandiose first-floor gallery and looking out over the park, where deer graze. Napoleon paid most of the price so that he could use Valençay Castle himself. In fact, he used it for six years to accommodate the Spanish king Ferdinand VII, who lost his throne through the emperor's fault. On regaining possession of the castle in 1814, Talleyrand refurbished the interior, and after the Congress of Vienna went to live there permanently with his niece by marriage, Dorothée, duchess of Dino. The grandiose palace, which has remained intact since the early 19th century, witnessed 20 years of balls, receptions, literary salons and meetings of the leading contemporary figures in politics and art.

274 bottom The halls of Valençay Castle contain antique furniture and original paintings, like the splendid oval frame containing the portrait of Princess Bénévent of Vigée-Lebrun.

275 top *The magnificent collection of paintings at Valençay includes a portrait of the famous minister Talleyrand (left), and one of Victoire Alexandrine Eléonore de Damas, countess of Talleyrand-Périgord, who lived in the late 18th century (center) and was the mother of Charles Maurice Talleyrand, portrayed by Prud'hon (right).*

*276 and 277
Talleyrand de Périgord
had to give up his lovely
residence at Valençay
between 1808 and
1814 to Ferdinand
VII, King of Spain,
who was exiled there
after being deposed by
Napoleon. Visitors
can see his chamber*
*(large photo), in First
Empire style, then
proceed along the
large gallery on the
first floor to other
magnificently
furnished rooms
like the Blue Room
(bottom left) and the
cabinet de toilette
(top right).*

278 and 279
Napoleon's prime
minister, Talleyrand
de Périgord, regained
possession of his castle
in 1814 and partly
renovated the interior
decoration. Some of
the most interesting
rooms are the ground-
floor hall containing
the table around
which the signatories
of the Congress of
Vienna sat (left-hand
page), the Great Hall
(top left), the Portrait
Gallery (top right),
and the Prince's
Chamber (bottom).

280 and 281 The Renaissance tower by Michelangelo's pupil, Fra Giocondo, and a window in flamboyant Gothic style stand out on the south façade of Meillant Castle. The defensive structure of the castle, which is still inhabited, can be clearly seen from the entrance moat. The building contains a wealth of furnishings, halls and chambers with painted coffered ceilings.

FRA GIOCONDO'S LOVELY TOWER: MEILLANT CASTLE

Meillant Castle, enveloped in the green mantle of the forest and the scent of lime trees in spring, reveals its pretty Gothic style with a lawn of strutting peacocks, glistening ponds and the "Lion" tower – a Renaissance construction by Michelangelo's pupil Fra Giocondo – that stands at the center of the façade. Remember this tower when viewing the more famous one at Blois Castle; the Italian Renaissance touch left the first trace of its brilliant harmony here. In fact, it was Charles II d'Amboise, lord of Chaumont and governor of Milan, who introduced into Meillant Castle discreet but perceptible signs of the art he had seen flourishing across the Alps. In the inner rooms, 17th-century Dutch furniture; a great banqueting hall with minstrel's gallery and tapestries made to a design by Raphael; and a spectacular dining room with a Renaissance fireplace, a gilded coffered ceiling (partly painted in bright colors) and Cordova leather wall hangings all bring to life the age of the duke of Charost, owner of the castle during the Revolution, who had a philanthropic bent. The epitaph on his tomb in the castle chapel states, "Everywhere and at all times he did nought but good."

282 top The impressive statue of Jacques-Coeur (left) stands in the heart of Bourges opposite the famous merchant adventurer's mansion (right); the Jacques-Coeur route, which takes in the major castles of the southern Loire region, is named after him.

282-283 In the austere rooms of La Chapelle d'Angillon Castle, author Alain-Fournier found his inspiration for the characters of his famous novels, including Le Grand Meaulnes.

THE LAND OF JACQUES-COEUR

The echoes of war give way to an ancient, bucolic landscape, while the Jacques-Coeur route continues north. After the calm sight of Apremont, the prettiest flowery village in France, comes Bourges, and the impressive statue in the town center of Jacques-Coeur, who gave the capital of Cher its most precious castle. Tall, handsome, and a lover of the sea and great ocean routes, he founded a shipping company whose sailing ships traveled far and wide to supply the king's court with spices, silks, silver, carpets and majolica. He financed Charles VII's military campaigns and was his private and most trusted banker until he fell into disgrace, it is said, because of the pretty Agnès Sorel, the king's mistress, and was thrown into prison. He escaped, embarked on a ship of the papal fleet that attacked the Turks, and died in 1456. His statue, which stands on a stone pedestal opposite the entrance, swathed in marble drapery, seems to admire his castle for eternity. In the heart of Henrichemont Forest, studded with pastures and clearings, castles are still the main leitmotiv. Maupas Castle is famous for its collection of 887 china plates from the oldest and most famous French pottery works, many of which hang on the walls alongside the wooden staircase, and for a silk tapestry of Italian manufacture given by the count of Chambord to the marquis of Maupas in the 19th century. Literary memories and the personalities invented by Alain-Fournier give a special appeal to the castle of La Chapelle D'Angillon. "I have returned to my land, the land that can only be seen by moving branches aside. I have never seen it so fresh, so concealed," wrote Alain-Fournier, when he was already beginning to imagine the adventures of *Le Grand Meaulnes* (published in English as *The Lost Domain*).

Cher, the department that, together with Indre, partly includes the ancient Berry, was a source of inspiration and peace for the author. He learned to read and write at the Epineuil-le-Fleuriel village school, enjoyed staying with his uncle in Nançay, a village comprising a few houses built around a single square, and daydreamed as a child in the great castle of La Chapelle D'Angillon. The dramatic destiny of the Princess of Clèves and the adventures of Le Grand Meaulnes, a young man lost in the memory of a mysterious kingdom where the enchanting Yvonne de Galais lived, accompany the visitor through the austere rooms of this castle. Alain-Fournier, the author of some famous novels, was born in 1886 in the village not far from the castle, but it was the great halls of the historic building that set light to his imagination. Two of them house relics of the writer's fantasy world, while others feature impressive fireplaces, beautiful paintings; a Luca della Robbia sculpture stands in the chapel, and a curious gallery is designed for *jeu de paume*, a fashionable game that was the forerunner of tennis.

283 top and center The castle of La Chapelle d'Angillon is one of the few mansions built in the Sologne area. Its severe look is inherited from the imposing original structure dating from the 11th century, while the central section was inspired by Renaissance architecture.

283 bottom Maupas Castle is famous for its collection of 887 china plates from the oldest and most famous French potteries, which adorn part of the wooden staircase and some of the rooms in this lovely residence.

SMALL WORLDS,
SPECIAL ATMOSPHERES

The land veined by the Cher River still encloses small worlds and an atmosphere of stillness: sleepy villages, roads that disappear into the countryside, abbeys, castles and landscapes untouched by the passage of time. The gentle countryside of Berry leads to the castle of La Verrerie. The Scots were at home here, because Charles VII gave this solitary castle to James Stuart in 1422. They kept it until 1683, when Louis XIV donated it to Countess Louise de Keroualle, Duchess of Portsmouth, and Charles II's mistress. In 1843 a descendent gave it to an ancestor of the present owners, the De Vogüé family. Nested in the greenery of Ivoy Forest is the classic castle with turrets, Renaissance porticoes, richly decorated halls, secret archives, huge, silent grounds, and a stream to provide silvery highlights. Visitors can admire the Gothic chapel, the reception rooms, the billiard room and the library. Some rooms are set aside for paying guests who wish to spend a night as a king amid velvets and canopies, ancestral portraits, tapestries and antique furniture. The world of fishing also appears on a royal frame. A few miles from Gien stands the lonely gray castle of La Buissière, already a fortress in the 12th century. Since 1962 the castle has housed the Fishing Museum, which contains exhibits of all kinds: fossil fish, silver fish, stuffed fish, sculpted fish, drawings of fish.

*284 and 285
The gentle Berry countryside and the thick Ivoy Forest surround La Verrerie Castle, with its Renaissance portico in the inner courtyard, and rooms furnished with antique furniture and damask fabrics. Some of the rooms are reserved for paying guests who would like to spend a night in the magical atmosphere of a great château.*

ANNE DE BEAUJEU'S RESIDENCE: GIEN CASTLE

The history of this small town, which stretches along the banks of the Loire, is closely linked to that of its castle, the first of those overlooking the Loire if the route of the famous river is followed towards the sea. The castle, standing high above the river at a point where the view is limitless, has offered hospitality to Joan of Arc among others. Before attending the coronation of Charles VII, the famous heroine spent a night praying in the wing of the castle now named after her, the only surviving part of the original feudal building.

The castle, overlooking Gien and the Loire, was built of brick and stone for Louis XI's daughter Anne de Beaujeu, Countess of Gien, in 1484. Francis I, Henri II, Charles IX and Henri III all stayed here. It survived unscathed the bombing of the Second World War, which razed the red-roofed town to the ground.

Since 1952 the castle has housed the Hunting Museum, which contains 15 rooms full of weapons of all ages, costumes, rare collections of buttons inspired by the hunt, works of art associated with the subject, tapestries, majolica, watercolors, lithographs, paintings by François Desportes, the famous animal painter to Louis XIV and Louis XV, and the Claude Hettier de Boislambert Collection of 500 hunting trophies. As well as the castle and its museum, Gien also offers another interesting attraction: the ceramic works founded in 1821 by Englishman Thomas Hulm, known as Hall, who wished to introduce the manufacture of fine English china into France. He found the right kind of clay for the purpose near Gien, while wood from the great forest of Orléans stoked the kilns that produced Gien blue, a color that remains inimitable today.

286 top Gien Castle, the first of the castles overlooking the Loire as the course of the famous river is followed, was built on the foundations of a hunting lodge erected for Charlemagne. Its involvement with hunting thus has ancient origins, and still continues today. The castle houses the magnificent Hunting Museum, which includes some lovely tapestries like the one woven following a cartoon by Laurent Guyot (right).

286 and 287 The large hall featuring paintings by François Desportes (1661–1743), with its mighty woodwork, contains numerous works by this famous animal painter who worked at the court of Louis XIV and Louis XV.

SULLY,
A ROMANTIC CASTLE

Sully Castle, a good example of defensive architecture on the border between Berry and Sologne, rises from the water like a romantic vision on the left bank of the Loire and its tributary, the Sange. The great hunting parties of yesteryear took place here, in the huge wooded Sologne Forest. The square tower at the entrance, the round tower on the southeastern side and the keep date back to the 15th century. From the knoll visitors can admire the castle, the park and the moats. Amid the greenery stands the marble statue of the duke of Sully, with a laurel wreath and the marshal of France baton. The Guard Room, with its coffered Vosges wood ceilings, leads to the Great Hall where Voltaire, exiled here after libeling the Prince Regent, Philippe d'Orléans, staged some of his plays between 1716 and 1719. Near the Great Hall, separated by a solid iron door, is the oratory, followed by the King's Chamber, with tapestries, a four-poster bed with blue canopy and wood-paneled walls. Finally, 40 steps lead up to the top floor, where visitors can see the framework of the roof: a brilliantly engineered wooden skeleton. This very tall pitched roof, which dates from the late 14th century, has undergone catapult attacks, but has always withstood them and is still there, like a great upside-down ship's hull, waiting to be admired for its latticework of beams and the unusual design of its roof.

288 and 289 The romantic sight of Sully Castle, a good example of defensive architecture, rises from the water on the border between Berry and Sologne. Among its attractions are the Guard Room, with its ceiling painted in pure gold, the King's Chamber – with tapestries portraying scenes from classical mythology and a blue damask canopy to match the walls – and the extraordinary roof frame, with its upturned-hull shape.

A WORLD
PRESERVED
IN STONE

Tourists who travel through the Loire Valley or merely hear stories about its magnificent residences wonder why so many castles and princely residences were built there. Why by the Loire, and not the Seine, for example, or other no less famous rivers? Because the Loire Valley, with its warm, dry climate, has always been the garden of France; because along the riverbanks there were already fortresses and castles able to accommodate royal guests; and because in the 15th century the king's political survival depended on the resistance offered along the Loire border by the dukes of Berry and Orléans in the south against the English and in the north against the Burgundians. Even after his accession to the throne, Charles VII remained fascinated by the climate and landscape of the gentle Loire Valley. After the Treaty of Troyes (1420), which stripped him of his kingdom, he lived at Chinon, Loches and Amboise with the sole title of Roi de Bourges. Following the legendary liberation by Joan of Arc of Orléans, besieged by the English, in May 1429, Charles VII began to win back his kingdom, but when he was finally able to return to liberated Paris on November 12, 1437, he only stayed a few days. Homesick, he took the court back to Chinon, preferring to pass his life in the gentle Touraine, where he had been bewitched by the beautiful Agnès Sorel. His son, Louis XI, who grew up at Loches Castle, though a restless wanderer by nature, nearly always lived in the castles of Amboise and Plessis-lez-Tours. Charles VIII, who was fond of Amboise, also had no desire to transfer the court to Paris.

After his marriage he spent a year at Langeais Castle; then, on his return from the Italian campaign in 1495, he decided to live at Amboise and convert the castle into a modern residence, for which purpose he summoned skilled craftsmen and artists from Italy. His successor, Louis XII, also chose the Loire, as did Francis I who lived at Blois Castle in the early years of his reign. Three years after his coronation began the construction of his own castle, Chambord. Today, in the summer, many castles stage historical reenactments; sound-and-light shows, pageants and plays to familiarize the public with the history of the best-known castles. The Francis I route follows the ancient road traveled by the king on his way to Italy, while the Vallée des Rois route leads to royal residences and sleepy old-world villages. Even without following a set route, the castles follow one after another. The castle of Chenonceau, the best known and most visited, recounts tales of love and the revenge of betrayed mistresses, while Villandry's charm focuses on its gardens. Cheverny is still inhabited, and the pack of dogs used for fox hunting in the autumn can be seen in its avenues in the afternoons.

Then there's Azay-le-Rideau; Langeais with its tapestries; Ussé, so unreal that it inspired the fairy tale of Sleeping Beauty; Blois, where French history was made and the duke of Guise was assassinated; Chinon, which featured in the destiny of Joan of Arc; Amboise, linked with Italy because of its association with Leonardo da Vinci; and Chambord, which, with its huge size, its 380 chimneys and 406 rooms, exemplifies and concludes the saga of the Loire castles.

290 top left Feudal towers and outer walls give Chaumont Castle, which stands on a hill overlooking the Loire, the appearance of an impregnable fortress. The castle has an air of mystery, the legacy of its association, at the height of its splendor, with a court astronomer who was more of a magician and fortune-teller than a scientist.

290 top right Villandry Castle is a magnificent residence, but its fame is not so much due to the interior as to its magnificent flower and vegetable gardens, whose colors change with the seasons and the crops. These gardens were inspired by ancient documents written by medieval monks.

290-291 Little Azay-le-Rideau Castle, framed by a romantic natural setting of rare beauty, overlooks the Indre River amid lush vegetation with plane trees, lime trees and tall oaks.

292 top The Salle des Gardes at Langeais Castle, with its classical layout and furnishings: great brass chandeliers, a pale stone fireplace, paneled walls and exposed beams on the ceiling.

THE INFLUENCE
OF ITALIAN ART

The Loire Valley is an immense setting that, in a way, belongs to the marvelous period of the Italian Renaissance. In the stone friezes, spiral staircases, windows lighting the halls, and castle porticoes – almost everywhere, in fact – Italian influence has left the unmistakable imprint of its grandeur. The façade of Valençay Castle has the same scenic perfection as the 15th century palazzi of Florence, the staircase of Blois Castle repeats the floral motifs of many Tuscan portals, and the names of many famous personalities are linked with the Loire Valley. One such personality was Catherine de Médicis who, when she married Henri II, brought to France the art of good living, the gaiety of the *volta* (a rather daring dance that delighted the court), and the elegance and taste of the great balls and banquets held in Florence under the Médicis.

Another was Leonardo da Vinci, who ended his days at the castle of Clos-Lucé in Amboise, given to him by Francis I. He arrived from Florence, his mules loaded with the canvases of the Mona Lisa, St. Anne and John the Baptist. He warmed himself by the fire in the Great Hall, and in the peace of that retreat organized magnificent parties for his French king, creating flying machines and robots that, when struck on the chest, released pure white lilies and perfumed roses onto the guests.

After his death and the return of Francis I from the Battle of Pavia (1528), the time was ripe for the king to return to the capital. The destiny of the Loire as the headquarters of the court was over. Chambord Castle was finished, and from then on was only used for holidays and hunting parties. However, distant sounds still seem to issue from that kingdom of keeps, pinnacles and parapets: the rustle of silk, the clank of armor, dance steps and the gentle notes of lutes and rebecs.

292-293 Standing alone at the end of a huge park, Chambord Castle incarnates the megalomaniac dream of a king who wished to conclude the age of the splendors and legends of the Loire Valley with the most magnificent castle ever built on the riverbanks.

293 right Blois Castle stands in the heart of the town of the same name on the right bank of the Loire, about 37 miles from Orléans. In the 15th century it was the favorite royal residence of Louis XII, who ordered large-scale extension work.

IN THE FOOTSTEPS OF JOAN OF ARC: CHINON CASTLE

Orléans commemorates Joan of Arc every May 8, when 1000 banners fly from Fort des Tourelles to Place St. Croix. The famous Maid of Orléans, played by a young girl, walks at the head of a great procession. This pageant commemorates the day in 1429 when Joan arrived to liberate the city from the English siege. Her "crusade" had set out from Chinon Castle, where Charles VII had taken refuge after escaping from Paris. Joan arrived there on March 9, 1429, escorted by six men, asking to be brought before the king. It was a dramatic time for France. Henry IV was king of England and king of Paris; Charles VII was only king of Bourges. The states general of the central and southern provinces, which had remained loyal to him, had decided to finance the war against the English, but the dauphin hesitated. Joan waited for two days, praying, until she was eventually received in the Throne Room (sadly now partly demolished; only the monumental fireplace remains, together with what, according to legend, is the footprint of the famous heroine). King Charles VII, who had exchanged clothes with a courtier, was concealed among 300 costumed nobles. But Joan was not to be deceived. She walked straight up to the king, embraced his knees and said, "My name is Joan, and I am sent by the king of Heaven to tell you that you will be crowned true king of the French at Rheims Cathedral." The king doubted her word and sent the girl to Poitiers for medical examinations, to establish whether she was a witch or an envoy of God. Eleven days later, convinced by the results, Charles VII permitted Joan of Arc to march at the head of his army against the English. Until 1450 Chinon Castle on the Vienne, a tributary of the Loire, was the headquarters of the court, which later moved to Amboise and Blois. The castle was used once more by Louis XII in 1498 to receive Cesare Borgia, sent by the Pope to deliver the papal bull annulling his marriage with Joan of France so that he could wed Anne of Brittany, thus uniting Brittany and France. The chronicles tell of a grandiose entrance of 68 mules bearing trunks, crates and chairs covered with gold brocade, accompanied by pages, minstrels and drummer-boys. Men and animals draped in brocades and crimson velvets preceded Duke Cesare, who rode a horse decked out with precious stones and pearls. The duke's costume was so precious and studded with gems and diamonds that it "shone like a lighthouse." The duke, son of the Pope, was received with full honors, although it was already known that as cardinal he had been his sister's lover and his brother's murderer. Little now remains of Chinon Castle apart from the grandiose foundations and some towers, including the Tour de l'Horloge with the bell, Marie Javelle, which has struck the hours since 1399, and the Tour d'Argenton, built towards the end of the 15th century, in the location where Louis XI is said to have held his prisoners.

The king's mistress, Agnès Sorel, lived in the adjacent Coudray Castle, which the sovereign reached via secret underground passages. Joan of Arc was held prisoner in the tower of the same building, as were the Templars, whose heartrending messages can still be read on the walls, centuries later. The countryside around Tours is characterized by precious vineyards that produce the red Chinon, Bourgeuil and Saint Nicolas and the white MontLouis and Vouvray wines that accompany the gastronomic delights of the Loire Valley.

294-295 Seen from the Vienne River, Chinon Castle reveals the defensive and military features of what was one of the most famous fortresses of the 15th century. Here the dauphin of France took refuge when he left Paris during a night of terror; Joan of Arc came to the castle too, to implore the king to grant her the honor of marching at the head of his troops against the English army besieging Orléans.

295 top Chinon, with its slate roofs and the web of narrow lanes at the foot of the castle, offers some major tourist attractions, such as a famous wine and a costume fair that, every August, takes the small town four centuries back in time.

295 right Built on a crag where the Romans had already established a castrum (camp) because of its strategic position on the river, Chinon Castle still has some towers that demonstrate that a veritable citadel, not just a castle, once stood at the summit of the village.

295 bottom Partly destroyed over the centuries, Chinon Castle is more famous for its magnificent architectural design than for its wealth of interior decorations, which include some magnificent Aubusson tapestries.

296-297 and 296 top Ussé Castle still breathes the enchanted atmosphere of Sleeping Beauty, the fairy tale by Charles Perrault that made it famous. Its towers, with their gray conical roofs, and the thick forest all around have helped preserve the magic of this spot over the centuries.

297 bottom The world-famous Ussé Castle is now a favorite destination of couples looking for a romantic setting for their wedding.

USSÉ: SLEEPING BEAUTY'S CASTLE

*U*ssé Castle, an enchanting mixture of pinnacles and pointed turrets, is known as Sleeping Beauty's castle. It was an ancient fortress when it belonged to Jean de Bueil, who married a daughter of Charles VII and Agnès Sorel. Work later began on converting it into a less severe home, bristling with towers and pinnacles. It was such an enchanted castle that it inspired Charles Perrault to write his famous fairy tale; so magical that it has caught the imagination of the Japanese, who travel halfway across the world to get married in this romantic setting. The castle is quadrangular in shape, bounded at the corners by keeps and pinnacles. However, like nearly all those in the Loire Valley, the appearance of the building and the original architectural plans, which date back to the 15th and early 16th centuries, were changed by the various owners. The interior of Ussé Castle is richly decorated, and its rooms, with their 18th-century tapestries and 17th- and 18th-century furniture, constitute veritable museums. Some tapestries also hang on the walls of the long gallery, with its black-and-white tiled floor. Paintings of famous schools line the main staircase and the Salle Royale. A rare piece of Renaissance furniture inlaid with ivory occupies almost an entire wall of the *cabinet florentin*. The chapel, which has a nave with no aisles, was built between 1523 and 1535. It contains 16th-century wooden choir-stalls and an enameled majolica Virgin attributed to Luca della Robbia.

297 top Two ancient cedars (legend has it that they were planted by Chateaubriand) protect the 16th-century chapel. The interior, which has a nave but no aisles, is decorated with wooden choir-stalls dating from the period when the chapel was built. However, the most valuable item is an enameled terracotta Madonna made by Luca della Robbia around the mid-15th century.

298 and 299 The wealth of the interior of Ussé Castle matches the charm of the exterior. The furnishings, especially the tapestries and furniture, enhance the magnificence of the 18th-century galleries and halls. The Aubusson tapestries and those by Flemish craftsmen depicting rural scenes are particularly exquisite. Ancient weapons and paintings of a good artistic level alternate with Italian furniture, like the rare ivory-inlaid specimen in the cabinet florentin.

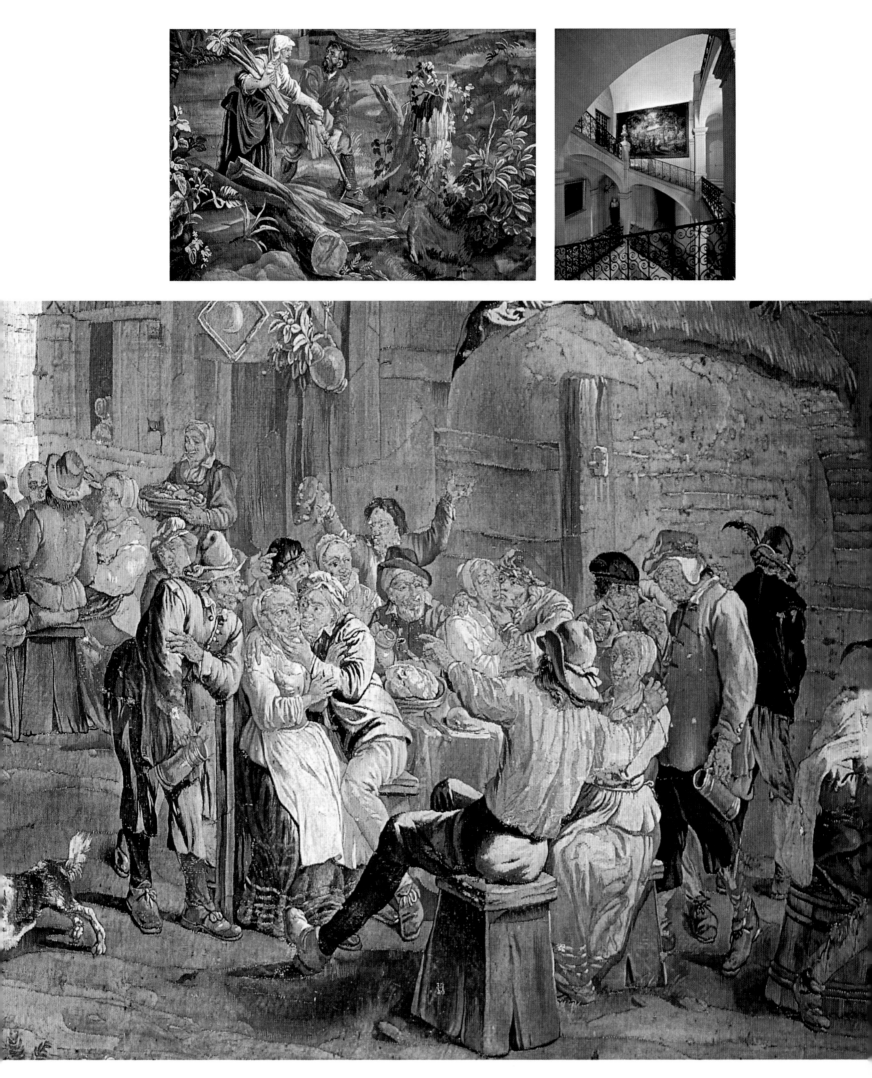

MORE TALES
OF LOVE AND WAR:
LOCHES CASTLE

etween one military campaign and the next, the sovereigns who lived by the Loire devoted a great deal of time to feasting, jousting and love affairs. They had mistresses whose names have gone down in history and who, in exchange for their loyalty, were rewarded with castles and riches. Charles VII and Agnès Sorel were bound by a true passion, and a castle was the reward for every child she bore (four in all). Loches Castle, the largest, had existed since the 6th century with the name of Castel-lum. In 840 Charles the Bald gave it to a loyal knight, who passed it on to a niece who married Foulques the Black of the House of Anjou. The castle has an exceptional defensive system of walls and towers. It underwent lengthy sieges in the 13th century in the battle fought for possession of Touraine between the Plantagenet King Henry II of England and his sons Richard the Lionheart and John Lackland against Philip Augustus. In the 15th century it became the favorite residence of Charles VII and Agnès Sorel. She died in 1450, and her body lies in an alabaster sarcophagus in the tower that bears her name. A portrait of the king's mistress in another room (a copy of the original, which is in a private collection) shows the delicate grace of her body and a naked breast escaping provocatively from the laces of a corset. From Loches it is just a short walk to Montrésor, one of the prettiest villages in France. The most famous lord of the manor was Imbert de Bastarnay, who bought the existing fortress in 1493 and converted it into the pretty castle that now belongs to the descendants of Count Branicki, the Polish nobleman who bought the property in the 19th century. A friend of Napoleon III, he was a leading financier and a collector of valuable works of art, now on display: paintings by Raphael, Caravaggio and Veronese, silverware belonging to the ancient kings of Poland, hunting trophies, jewelry and furniture from the Italian Renaissance period.

300-301 and 301 top
The warm light of sunset mellows the austere design of Loches Castle. More of a defensive bulwark than a romantic castle, it has survived intact over the centuries, with its famous tower, the royal gate, and the chancellery built by the Counts of Anjou. The Counts, who were among the first owners of the castle, also ruled over the town, with its narrow medieval lanes huddled at the foot of the crag.

302 top left Huge fireplaces, shining armor and splendid windows give the interior of the castle a unique, fascinating atmosphere.

302 bottom right It was in this room that Joan of Arc delivered her famous speech to King Charles VII in June 1429, urging him to go to Rheims to be crowned king of the French.

302-303 The beautiful Agnès Sorel had a long love affair with Charles VII. Her tomb, watched over by an angel, lies in a tower of the castle.

303 bottom Pages of history have been written at Loches Castle, from the long love affair between Charles VII and the lovely Agnès Sorel to the imprisonment of Cardinal La Balue, counselor to Louis XI, who betrayed the king

to Charles the Bold. He was imprisoned in the Martelet, the gloomy prison with three tiers of cells (cachots) constructed in the Tour Neuve, where Ludovico il Moro, duke of Milan, was also held prisoner by Louis XII.

304-305 and 304 top
Saumur Castle, a
quadrangle bounded
by polygonal towers
with conical slate
roofs, stands on a
rocky promontory
that seems to watch
over the last stretch of
the Loire as it flows
towards the sea.

THE CASTLES OF ANJOU

Here the Loire enters Anjou, and before reaching the sea passes by two more famous castles, those of Saumur and Angers. The castle of Saumur, the town that contains the leading French riding school, stands on a rocky promontory. The castle, a quadrilateral with polygonal corner towers, conical roofs of bluish slate and Renaissance-Gothic decorations on a visibly medieval structure, is reached by walking up narrow, steep streets, until the effort is rewarded by a superb view and a visit to the richly decorated rooms. The castle dates from the late 14th century, although its appearance reveals some later additions.

It was the Italian Bartolomeo who built the outer fortifications, which herald the form of the typical Vauban ramparts. A Huguenot stronghold in the 17th century, then a barracks and a penitentiary, it was restructured at the turn of this century and houses three museums: the Decorative Arts Museum, Toy Soldier Museum and Equestrian Museum, which displays harnesses, trappings and uniforms.

Although it has the resources and dynamism of a big city, Angers, with its close-knit network of squares and pedestrian precincts and its clusters of houses over 500 years old, looks like a large village. At the center is its symbol: the squat pentagonal fortress erected by Blanche of Castille, mother of St. Louis, in the early 13th century as a bulwark against the restless Breton populations. Later, at the end of the 13th century, residential buildings, hanging gardens and a chapel for the ducal family of Anjou were added. What was once the residence of the poet-prince René contains the famous *Apocalypse*, about 118 yards of allegorical scenes made with the tapestry technique by 14th-century artists. It has six sections, each divided into 14 episodes, featuring red-blue shades, dragons with huge heads, quadrupeds ridden by Death, sea creatures with macabre features and crude representations of the human face. This is the best visiting card for the itinerary that starts from the castle and continues as far as the "*promenade du bout du monde,*" leading the visitor to the attractive historic buildings in the town center.

305 left and top right Saumur Castle dates from the late 14th century, but like all those in the famous valley it was altered over the centuries and also served various purposes: it was a Huguenot stronghold in the 17th century, then a barracks, and then a penitentiary. It now houses three museums: the Decorative Arts Museum, the Toy Soldier Museum and the Equestrian Museum.

305 bottom right The mighty Angers Castle, a squat pentagonal fortress, was built by Blanche of Castille, mother of Saint Louis, in the early 13th century, to protect the area, which was threatened by the restless Breton populations.

A LADY'S ROMANTIC DREAM: AZAY-LE-RIDEAU

306 and 307 The greenery of the park contrasts with the silvery veil of the Indre River as it flows past Azay-le-Rideau Castle, creating a romantic atmosphere. An enchanting blend of pinnacles and sharp turrets, the castle houses valuable works of art such as a 16th-century portrait by an unknown artist of a young woman reading, a portrait of Louis XIV standing, and a 16th-century portrait of the duke of Guise, nicknamed le Balafré (Scarface).

*I*n the spot where the road from Tours to Chinon crosses the Indre, a left-hand tributary of the Loire, once stood the watchtower of Azay-le-Rideau. This was a medieval fortification surrounded by a deep moat and manned by a garrison of Burgundian soldiers. For 100 years it was no more than a pile of rubble, after Charles VII set fire to the entire village and the fortified tower in 1418, also killing the soldiers of the garrison, to take revenge for the insults he had received. In 1518 the court financier, Gilles Berthelot, treasurer to Francis I, bought the property and commissioned architect Étienne Rousseau to erect a castle in Renaissance style in a pretty spot where the Indre formed a small lake. The work lasted 10 years, until 1529, and was directed by the financier's wife, Philippa Lesbahy. The result was a residence designed for the pure pleasure of living in it, with no defensive purposes. It was built partly on the water, its romantic white image reflected in the lake, with conical towers, slate roofs and pretty ornaments outside and the great right-angled staircase inside. It was Philippa Lesbahy who gave the residence the elegant furnishings it still retains: drawing rooms full of paintings, a collection of blue majolica plates, and walls hung with Gobelin tapestries. That is why the castle is one of the most beautiful in the Loire Valley and was liked so much by Francis I who, taking advantage of a

conspiracy, had no hesitation in confiscating it and exiling the owner, Berthelot. In the King's Chamber, where Francis I almost certainly stayed, is a great fireplace with the initials F and C (standing for queen Claude). It is followed by the Green Room, named after the huge green damask four-poster bed dating from the 17th century, the Red Room, where crimson damask still prevails in the furnishings, and the Banqueting Hall, with its huge fireplace and valuable Brussels tapestries.

306

308 and 309 Great
tapestries hang from
the walls of the
magnificent
Renaissance-style
rooms of Azay-le-
Rideau Castle,
featuring great
fireplaces, light,
vaulted kitchens and
a simple but elegant
main staircase
leading to the upper
floors. It was Mme
Philippa Lesbahy in
the 16th century who
gave the castle the
gentle, cozy air it still
retains today.
Designed as a
medieval fortification,
it was reduced to a
pile of ruins in 1418,
and finally converted
to a nobleman's
residence in 1529.

310 More beautiful rooms in Azay-le-Rideau castle bear witness to the famous personalities who stayed there: the Salle à Manger, decorated in Henri II style (top right), the chamber of Francis I with the royal emblem of the salamander engraved on the fireplace (left), and the Blue Room (bottom right), which belonged to Maréchal de la Barre, who was killed in the siege of Nice in 1705.

311 A plain four-poster bed, an original marble table, wall hangings and golden yellow curtains with the most popular flower patterns, and a monumental fireplace are the few concessions to luxury in the simple, cozy bedroom of Francis I.

A CASTLE OF WEAPONRY AND LOVE: LANGEAIS

312 The marriage of
Charles VIII to Anne
of Brittany was
celebrated in Langeais
Castle in 1491. The
hall where the
wedding took place,
with its great
tapestries and beamed
ceiling, remains intact
(bottom right). The
royal bedchamber,
with its four-poster bed
(bottom left),
exemplifies the
furnishings typical of
great 15th-century
mansions. In
Langeais Castle, 13
chambers are hung
with 15th- and 16th-
century Flemish
tapestries. The chapel
(top left) has the
typical inverted-hull-
shaped ceiling.

*I*n the numerous castles that follow the Loire Valley from Gien to Saumur, the desire for beauty replaced the need for defensive security in the century of the Renaissance. Langeais Castle, situated to the west of Tours by the riverside, is the only medieval fortress that has remained intact and has never been changed over the centuries by rebuilding work. After passing through the main door visitors enter the inner courtyard, where they see the ruins of a high wall, part of the ancient fortress built in 994 by Foulques the Red, founder of the Anjou Dynasty, a farsighted politician and strategist, but also a treacherous, cynical feudal brigand.

Langeais Castle and the entire province of Touraine passed to the Counts of Anjou in the 11th century, then to the Plantagenets. During the Hundred Years' War it was occupied by the English on various occasions. The present castle was built by Louis XI. Charles VIII and Anne of Brittany were married there in 1491. The chronicles tell of the magnificent procession that escorted the future bride, clad in a gold and velvet robe decorated with 160 sables, into the king's presence, and of the magnificent banquet with flocks of doves, meat pies, patties containing warblers, quails and turtle doves, and boiled capons covered with fine gold. After the wedding the severe feudal castle must have seemed gloomy to the 15-year-old bride, who only a year later preferred to move with the court to Amboise Castle. Since then, Langeais Castle has never reappeared in the history books, but the austere style of its walls, the rooms hung with 16th-century tapestries and the valuable antique furniture beautifully recreate the atmosphere of its legendary past.

313 Proud and solemn
in its feudal armor,
Langeais Castle has
survived the ravages
of time and war
unharmed. The castle,
whose features are
typical of late 15th-
century defensive
architecture, overlooks
the Loire and the roofs
of the village below.

*314 and 315
Medieval and
Renaissance styles are
blended in the
majestic Amboise
Castle, with its stone
friezes, spiral
staircases and
windows casting light
on halls and
porticoes. Standing
high above the Loire,
the castle still seems to
control its strategic
position as a defensive
bulwark by the ford.
For centuries that
was its function, with
the result that its
walls have witnessed
a great deal of
history.*

Amboise Castle is one of the most important castles in the Loire Valley because of the historical events that took place there and the role it played in introducing Italian art into France. Its origins date from the Gallo-Roman period. In 500 Clovis, king of the Franks, met Alaric, king of the Visigoths, there. They challenged one another to a chivalrous duel, and Alaric was killed. Later, the importance of Amboise grew with the construction of the bridge over the Loire, because there were only seven bridges between Gien and Angers, and anyone who controlled them, thus enabling

troops to cross the river, would control the entire region.

The promontory of Chatelliers, a spur of rock at the end of which stands Amboise Castle, was always a crossroads because of its ideal position at the confluence of the Loire and the Amasse. The bridge, town and castle were owned by the Counts of Amboise until the mid-15th century, when Charles VII ordered them to be confiscated in favor of his son Louis XI, who took up residence there with his wife, Charlotte of Savoy. Thus Charles VIII, who became king at the age of 13 and was already a courageous commander by the age of 20, was born at Amboise. On his return from the Italian campaign in 1494 he brought with him not only furniture, carpets and fabrics but also Italian artists, painters, tailors and craftsmen who soon changed the face of the castle. Amboise was transformed.

Landscape gardener Pacello Mercogliano created the first Italianate garden; brilliant architects and sculptors embellished the residence in accordance with Renaissance style; and hundreds of Turkish carpets and tapestries from Flanders and Damascus adorned the magnificent rooms.

A solemn tournament was held to celebrate its renovation. On April 7, 1498, Easter Eve, Charles VIII, accompanied by his wife, Anne of Brittany, went to the Hacquelebac Gallery on the way to the tournament field. Charles forgot to bend his head, and though he was by no means tall, he accidentally hit his forehead against the entrance architrave. He still watched the tournament, but then fell into a coma and died at 9 o'clock the same evening. He was succeeded by his cousin Louis d'Orléans, who became King Louis XII, married Charles' widow, Anne of Brittany, and gave Amboise to Louise of Savoy, mother of Francis I of Angoulême, who was heir to the throne. When he became king in 1515, Francis I demonstrated a particular fondness for the castle where he had spent his childhood. He completed the wing begun by Louis XII and summoned Leonardo da Vinci from Italy.

318-319 Magnificent
furnishings and
original paintings
decorate the rooms of
Amboise Castle, like
the room in Louis
Philippe style
dominated by crimson
fabrics and upholstery.

319 The hall is
dominated by the
great portraits
hanging on the walls,
including those of the
duke of Orléans (top
left) and Maria
Amelia of Bourbon
(top right).

320 top *The elegant Salle aux Poutres, designed and decorated between the 15th and 16th centuries, contains exquisite tapestries, beamed ceilings and priceless antique furniture.*

320 left and 321 top and bottom *The classic, severe style of the Renaissance period dominates these rooms of Amboise Castle; a good example is provided by the chamber of Henri II, with the large tapestries on the walls, great fireplaces, and four-poster beds.*

320-321 The classical style of furnishing characteristic of all the Loire chateaux can be seen in the Salle des Gardes, with its Gothic ceilings, and the rooms adjacent to it.

322 and 323 Amboise Castle not only provided the venue for some major historical events; above all, it provided the base from which Renaissance art was introduced into France because the great Leonardo da Vinci (shown here in a marble bust at top left) moved from Milan to spend the rest of his life there. His tomb is in St. Hubert's Chapel, constructed in flamboyant Gothic style with large windows and a richly decorated portal.

324 and 325 After loading some precious canvases, including the Mona Lisa, onto mules, Leonardo da Vinci left Florence for Amboise at the age of 64. Here Francis I is shown awaiting the great artist, to whom he donated Clos-Lucé Castle, where he spent the rest of his life.

His spirit can be felt in every room, such as the bedroom with the four-poster bed and large stone fireplace where he died, and in the collection on the basement of scale models of brilliant machines that he designed and about which he left detailed notes.

AN ARTIST'S JOURNEY AND A KING'S FRIENDSHIP LEONARDO DA VINCI AND FRANCIS I: FROM AMBOISE TO CLOS-LUCÉ

Leonardo, at the age of 64, loaded the canvases of the Mona Lisa, St. Anne and John the Baptist onto mules, left Florence, and set off for Amboise with his faithful disciple, Francesco Melzi, and his servant, Battista di Villanis. Francis I received the Italian genius at Amboise, and gave him Cloux Castle (now Clos-Lucé) and an annuity of 700 gold scudos. All he required in exchange was the pleasure of conversation with him. From 1516, Leonardo spent the last years of his life in the Loire Valley, masterminding splendid parties, masked balls and artists' conferences, and continuing his studies of engineering and anatomy. He lies in St. Hubert's Chapel in Amboise Castle. On the death of Francis I in 1547, the decline of Amboise began. In the 17th century Louis XIII visited the castle to hunt in the nearby forest, but under Louis XIV the mighty walls became grim state prisons. Amboise castle regained its past glory under Louis XV, who gave it to the duke of Choiseul, and later under Napoleon, who confiscated the castle and gave it to a member of the Directory, Roger Ducos. The latter had insufficient funds to maintain the great building and demolished part of it, but despite this mutilation, the castle still presents a faithful picture of what court life must have been like 400 years ago. There were two mighty towers, about 22 yards tall, with spiral staircases, in which a horse could be ridden right to the top; the king's apartments, the guardroom, and a wonderful view from the large terrace over the Loire and its tributary, the Amasse, complete the picture of one of the most spectacular castles in the valley. A long walk from Amboise is the magic of Clos-Lucé Castle, the residence of Leonardo da Vinci. The king and the "painter-cum-engineer" got along extraordinarily well; both of them enthusiastically cherished fantastic dreams. Leonardo was planning to build prefabricated wooden houses for the populace, to connect all the Loire castles with a series of canals, to make flying machines with wings. His designs and intuitions were ahead of their time in a century of humanists not given to flights of fancy. The time was not yet ripe for the scientific innovations that continually issued from the mind of the great genius, and everything remained on paper. At Clos-Lucé, in the very rooms that witnessed this outpouring of ideas and the long talks between the Italian artist and his royal patron, the astonished visitor can view the collection of manuscripts and the models of machines reconstructed in accordance with Leonardo's detailed instructions.

326-327 and 326 top
Magic and mystery
inhabit Chaumont
Castle, with its pale
stone and sloping
slate roofs, situated
just a few miles from
Amboise and Blois,
which were so
powerful in the
Middle Ages.

A QUEEN'S DARK SECRETS: CHAUMONT

The memory of Catherine de Médicis pervades the halls of Chaumont Castle. In 1560, as widow of Henri II, she bought the castle to take her revenge for her husband's adultery and force his mistress, Diane de Poitiers, to exchange it for Chenonceau Castle, which Henri had given her in 1547, when he ascended to the throne. The beautiful Diane could hardly refuse, but did not stay long at Chaumont, preferring exile at Anet Castle, where she died seven years later, far from the gossip of the Loire Valley.

The memory of the great Catherine is still very much alive at Chaumont. Her adviser on the occult arts, the sorcerer Ruggieri, is said to have stayed there, and the existence of a room connected to a tower by a steep staircase has led to rumors of a secret hideaway where the queen and her adviser retired to conduct magic rites and interrogate the stars about the future. Catherine is said to have discovered the tragic destiny awaiting her three children and the imminent advent of the Bourbons at Chaumont. The castle stands on a hill overlooking the left bank of the river. Until the 15th century it was the feudal fortress of the Counts of Blois; it was later rebuilt with round guard towers and softened by the addition of conical roofs and Renaissance influences. It passed through the hands of various owners, including the chatelain who demolished the north wing in the 18th century to obtain a better view of the Loire, and one Le Ray who, also in the 18th century, arranged for the famous Italian pottery maker Battista Nini to stay there. The latter set up his workshop in the stables, and his great kiln in an old dovecote. He made an important contribution to the history of art by reproducing numerous copies of ceramic medallions of the most famous personalities of the period, some of which are on display in the rooms of the castle leading to the chambers of Diane, Catherine and the astrologer Ruggieri.

328 The air of mystery with which Chaumont Castle was rife soon became a legend; the main centers from which this fascination still radiates are the chamber of Queen Catherine de Médicis (bottom right) in her favorite green, that of the sorcerer Ruggieri (top right), and the chapel, with its pointed stained-glass windows (top left).

329 The narrow Gothic-style staircase that runs through the heart of the castle perhaps led to the mysterious laboratory of the occult arts presided over by Ruggieri, the powerful court astrologer who predicted the death of Henri III, which put an end to the reign of the Valois dynasty.

330 and 331 Though it boasts three main buildings, a keep and a court of honor, Villandry Castle does not tell the stories of kings and queens. Spanish magnate Carvallo came to Villandry after the Second World War with the intention of buying the ancient castle to create a special garden. The rooms, with the original marble checkerboard floor (bottom right), can be visited, and the architectural design of the mighty building admired, but then the visitor will inevitably be drawn to the flower gardens, the avenues lined with lime trees and the unusual vegetable garden (top left).

IN BALZAC'S LOVELY COUNTRYSIDE: VILLANDRY

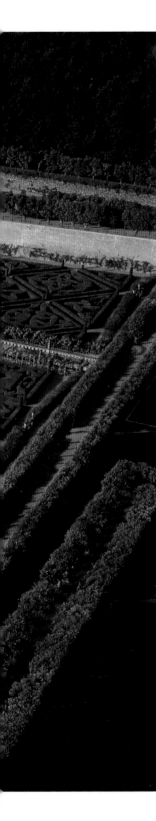

Nature reigns supreme in the quiet Touraine; meadows and forests play with the silvery ribbon of the river that flows, murmurs and splashes in the royal gardens and penetrates everywhere, constituting the characteristic feature of the gentle, sunny landscape of the Loire Valley. The charm of Villandry Castle revolves around its unique gardens. The history of France has never entered its walls, nor was it ever the home of a king or a courtesan. It was built about 10 miles from Tours by Jean le Breton, prime minister of Francis I, in 1536. He constructed three horseshoe-shaped buildings opening onto the Loire Valley on the foundations of a feudal fortress that was demolished, and of which only the south keep remains. Cross windows, dormer windows with carved pediments and tall, steeply sloping slate roofs form a complex of rare harmony, although the turrets and pinnacles have not survived. A simpler style, which was later to become the Henri IV style, was beginning to predominate in monumental architecture. However, the history of the castle is of little importance at Villandry. It is the square gardens, arranged by color and obsessively well tended, that invite the visitor to roam among terraces, kitchen gardens and flower beds whose colors change from season to season. The layout of the gardens was restored to its original 16th-century design by Spanish millionaire Carvallo, who became the castle's owner after the

Second World War. After discovering the original designs by Androuet du Cerceau, the architect who created the gardens, Carvallo recreated the original structure, with three terraces built on different levels, avenues shaded by lime trees, straight paths along which flowers blossom, box hedges clipped by topiarists and the curious herbariums of the medieval monks; visitors can stroll through the garden of love and the garden of music, amid mallow and chervil, beets, cabbage seedlings and pumpkins.

333 The ornamental gardens dedicated to love are clearly seen from the panoramic terrace. The designer intended the arrangement of the hedges to reflect the symbols of various types of love: hearts and flames represented tender love, deformed hearts delirious love, swords and daggers tragic love, and fans and letters of the alphabet elusive love.

332 Androuet du Cerceau designed the gardens of Villandry, magnificent green spaces that still retain their original appearance, with three terraces built at different levels. The layout of the gardens not only reflects the taste of the period, but also aims to recreate a philosophical symbolism in the arrangement of hedges and floral decorations. Some very rare species, often from distant regions, were cultivated here in the 16th century.

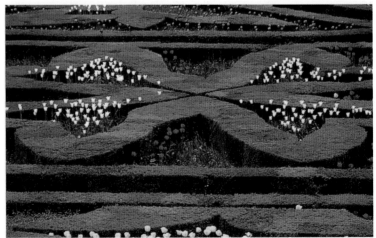

334 Chenonceau was built for Catherine Briçonnet, given to Diane de Poitiers (portrayed as Diana the Huntress by Primaticcio, bottom left) by her lover Henri II (shown in a contemporary portrait, bottom left), reclaimed by Catherine de Médicis, and passed on to Louise of Lorraine, widow of Henri III, who spent 12 years mourning there.

THE CASTLE OF QUEENS: CHENONCEAU

Just a stone's throw from the flourishing, idyllic rural town of Montrichard stands the most frequently visited and most romantic castle in the Loire Valley: Chenonceau, known as "the castle of six ladies" because of the role played by six chatelaines in its 400-year history. This *caprice des femmes* is famous for its five-span bridge and the two-storey gallery over the Cher, as well as the 15th-century circular keep, the gardens dedicated to Catherine and Diane, the two women who shared the king's favors, and the interior, including Diane de Poitiers' room, Catherine de Médicis' green study, and the queen's chamber, decorated with Gobelin tapestries. At different times the castle was inhabited by Mme. Catherine Briconnet, who built it with her husband, Thomas Bohier, Diane de Poitiers, who was given it by her lover Henri II, Catherine de Médicis, who reclaimed it on her husband's death, and Louise of Lorraine, widow of Henri III, who mourned her husband's death there, dressed in white according to royal protocol; she is said to have murmured nothing but prayers for 12 years.

After Louise of Lorraine, Chenonceau fell into a period of decline until Mme Dupin became its owner in the 18th century, and one of the most famous literary salons of the age developed around her and Jean-Jacques Rousseau, her son's tutor. In 1864 the castle was bought by Mme Pelouze, who meticulously restored its original design and then sold it to the present owners, the Menier family.

The grace of its design, the airy beauty of the gallery built by Catherine de Médicis and the tidy grounds once provided the romantic setting for the lives of queens and courtesans, which are recreated every summer evening in a sound-and-light show.

335 So ethereal that it seems to glide through the blue waters of the Cher like a stone galleon, so rich in history that every corner of the expansive grounds and halls evoke the ghosts of the ladies who lived, suffered, rejoiced and intrigued between the walls there, Chenonceau is one of the most famous castles in France.

336 The rooms of the castle are richly decorated, as they must have been at the height of its glory: some good examples are the large kitchen (bottom right), the Gothic gallery with its ogival vaults (left) and the chamber of Gabrielle d'Estrée, King Henri IV's mistress (top right).

336-337 Pure gold and crimson tapestries decorate Louis XIII's chamber, with its magnificent fireplace and the portrait of Louis XIV attributed to Rigaud and set off by a magnificently carved and gilded frame. On the right can be seen the great fireplace with the symbols of the ermine and the salamander, belonging to Francis I and his bride, Claude de France.

337 top The gallery, illuminated by 18 windows ordered by Catherine de Médicis for court banquets, was used as a hospital during the First World War.

337

338 top
The Chambre des Reines is a delightful blend of style and luxury; the room is dominated by Diane de Poitiers' bed, which, according to legend, had an "extraordinary" effect on those who reclined in it.

338 left Italian furniture appeared in French palaces as early as the 16th century. The item shown in this photo, decorated with ivory and mother-of-pearl, is the work of 15th-century Florentine craftsmen.

339 Diane de Poitiers' bedroom, known as the Chambre des Reines, contains two impressive Flemish tapestries of rare beauty (the one in the picture above portrays scenes from court life) and a massive fireplace decorated with the royal symbols in pure gold (right photo).

338-339 The chamber of César de Vendôme, son of Henri IV and Gabrielle d'Estrée, who owned the castle in the 17th century, contains a wealth of gold and tapestries.

CRIME, INTRIGUE AND COURTLY LOVE: BLOIS

340 and 341 Much of the history of France has passed through this castle, built by the Counts of Blois in the 14th century as a bridgehead on the Loire. However, only a few relics survive of the ancient feudal building, onto which the restorations and alterations commissioned by Charles d'Orléans, Louis XII and Francis I were grafted.

"Great souls," wrote Victor Hugo, "have left faint traces of their memory at Blois Castle." Its complex history has given the grandiose construction various styles, from the flowery Gothic of the façade to the Renaissance style of the famous staircase and the classical look of the Gaston d'Orléans wing. In the 14th century this medieval building, designed as a bridgehead on the Loire, belonged to the Counts of Châtillon, the last of whom sold it in 1391 to Duke Louis d'Orléans,

brother of Charles VI. When the duke was killed in Paris by the Burgundian John the Fearless, the castle passed into the hands of Charles d'Orléans, the family poet. Taken prisoner at the battle of Azincourt, Charles was incarcerated for 25 years, comforted by poetry and great literature. When he was released at the end of the Hundred Years' War, Charles d'Orléans thought no more of battle. At the age of 50 he fell in love with the 14-year-old Marie de Clèves, married her and went back to live at Blois Castle, surrounded by writers, artists and an army of architects who demolished the old fortress and erected a stone and brick building.

The complex, with its magnificent Renaissance staircase, was embellished by Francis I, who ascended to the throne in 1515, married Claude de France, by whom he had seven children, and built the famous staircase and the splendid fireplaces. Catherine de Médicis gave an aura of mystery to the royal apartments; behind secret

342 bottom
The Renaissance tower
and Louis XII wing
also overlook the inner
courtyard, producing
a monumental
ensemble of rare beauty.
The effect is enhanced
by niches like the one

shown here. Appearing
on the main castle
door is this Gothic-
style equestrian statue
of Louis XII,
decorated by the classic
Capetian fleurs-de-lys
and a frieze depicting
a porcupine.

342-343 Blois reached
the height of its power
in the 12th and 13th
centuries, and
continued to play an
important role in
French political life
until the 17th century.
In the 18th century,

before the Revolution,
the town and castle
attracted the interest
of many French artists.
This watercolor, by
Henri Joseph Van
Blarenberghe, dates
from the late 18th
century.

doors in her study she concealed precious documents, her famous pearl necklace and, so it was rumored, bottles of poison. Catherine de Médicis' hideaway, which has remained almost intact, still features 237 carved wooden panels that conceal cupboards that can only be opened by pressing a pedal concealed in a plinth. Francis II, Charles IX and Henri III reigned at Blois between 1547 and 1574, directed by their able mother, Catherine de Médicis. The history of the castle recommenced under Henri III. The States General were convened in the huge hall on the ground floor in 1576 to demand the suppression of the Huguenot religion. The States General were again convened in 1588 by Duke Henri de Guise who, supported by the king of Spain, attempted to depose the king. But before going down to the hall where he was expected, Henri III arranged for his rival to be led into a trap and stabbed. The king watched the murder from his chamber. Eight months later, he was to meet the same fate by the hand of Jacques Clément. Until 1617, when Louis XIII sent his mother, Maria de Médicis, into exile there, Blois played no part in history. However, Maria did not stay long. One night, after two years of boredom, she, despite her bulk, climbed down a rope ladder from the window; her son had no choice but to reconcile with his mother after her adventurous escape. However, by then Louis XIII had discovered that Blois, which was quite

a long way from Paris, made an excellent gilded prison. In 1626 he sent his brother Gaston d'Orléans there, promising him sufficient funds to build a residence worthy of his rank. Gaston, forgetting his love of political conspiracy, had the architect Mansart draw up plans for a castle, which required the demolition of the existing wings. For three years, work on a new wing opposite the main door in the courtyard proceeded apace. Then, after the birth of Louis XIV, the danger that Gaston might inherit the throne of France receded; Cardinal Richelieu cut off the funds and the work came to a halt. Gaston, dissatisfied with the new section he had built, went to live in the Francis I wing, and devoted his time to collecting rare plants.

343 top left
The influence exerted in France by the discovery of the Italian Renaissance is due to Francis I, who conducted a military campaign in Italy; this influence is particularly evident in the staircase of the Francis I wing in the inner courtyard of Blois Castle.

343 top right
The Gaston d'Orléans wing (the magnificent staircase of which can be seen in this photo) overlooks the inner courtyard. Work on this wing began in 1635 and lasted for three years, until Cardinal Richelieu cut off the funds required.

344 top Visitors can once again follow in the footsteps of Catherine de Médicis at Blois Castle. Her chamber is rich in gold work and luxurious "trifles," such as the four-poster bed and the unusual floor with its gilded tiles framed with the ever-present fleur-de-lys.

344-345 From
Catherine's bedroom,
access is obtained to
her private hideaway,
its walls covered with
fake panels made of
wood and pure gold
that conceal secret
hiding places.

345 top left and
bottom As at
Chenonceau, the most
luxurious furniture at
Blois came from Italy.
Tuscan craftsmen, in
particular, were very
popular in the 15th
and 16th centuries.

345 right Scenes
from court life were
immortalized by
artists of the period,
as in this tondo by
Ulysse Besnard, which
shows Catherine de
Médicis receiving
some ambassadors.

346 top left and bottom The salamander motif, emblem of Francis I, appears in the friezes on the fireplaces and in the furniture made specially for the king.

346 top right This portrait shows Marguerite of Navarre, known as Queen Margot, the sister of King Henri III of France.

346-347 More halls, chambers and galleries of the grandiose Blois Castle, with fireplaces bearing the initials and symbols of Francis I and Claude de France, Renaissance furniture and portraits; the wall decorations, however, are typical of the late 19th and early 20th centuries.

347 top Another 39 historical portraits from the French royal court, as well as Margot's, crowd the gallery in the Louis XII wing.

347 bottom The busts of Henri II, Henri III, Henri IV and Charles IX have been placed in the Galerie des Loges, among magnificent pieces of ivory-inlaid Italian furniture and tapestries of the Flemish school.

348 top The portrait of Louis XIV attributed to Hyacinthe Rigaud pays homage to one of the most powerful French monarchs in history; however, Louis XIV never spent even a day at Blois Castle.

348-349 Blois Castle presents the set patterns of what was once the classic style of castle furnishing: the King's Room, with its four-poster bed, the great fireplaces in every room, coffered ceilings and tapestries hanging from the walls.

349 top This picture shows a detail of the beautiful tapestry hanging in the bedroom of Henri III; the three fleurs-de-lys, the king's initial and the royal crown are recognizable.

349 bottom The windows of the Salle des États bear symbols of the Capetian dynasty's power; on the left is the ermine, the emblem of Anne of Brittany, and on the right the porcupine, emblem of Louis XII.

350 and 351 Blois Castle witnessed the ruthless murder of Henri de Guise, treacherously killed by order of King Henri III.

The King's Chamber evokes that tragic December 23, 1588, also immortalized in two famous 19th-century canvases.

352 top left The small Beauregard Castle contains a gallery of 327 portraits, unique in the history of the Loire châteaux. The portraits in the long Galerie des Illustres include that of Henry IV on horseback.

352-353 Beauregard Castle, nestled in Russy Forest, is cradled by the calm Beuvron Valley.

THE CHARM OF GREAT MANSIONS: BEAUREGARD AND CHEVERNY

*L*uxuriant, restful countryside leads from Blois to nearby Beauregard Castle, situated at the end of a long drive that cuts through Russy Forest. This small, secluded private castle, its dimensions still as perfect as when it was commissioned in the 16th century by Jean du Thier, secretary of state to Henri II, is worth a visit for its rooms, the large kitchen decorated as in ancient times, and the gallery containing 327 portraits of famous personalities, which is unique in the history of the Loire castles. This Galerie des Illustres was installed by Paul Ardier in the large first-floor gallery that once contained an attractive 16th-century white marble fireplace. The personalities portrayed are prelates, kings, queens, professors and military commanders spanning two centuries. Some pretty delft tiles in the characteristic blue and white colors, laid along the walls in 1628, decorate the austere row of characters hanging side by side, who recount the history of France. At nearby Cheverny Castle, dating from the 17th century, it is the charm of a great mansion, inhabited for 300 years by the family of the marquises of Vibraye and their successor, viscount of Sigelas, that enchants visitors, who can view its magnificent library, painted halls, grandiose weapons room and a collection of 2,000 hunting trophies. The pack of fox-hunting dogs barking excitably from the kennels on one side of the castle recall the great hunting tradition of the castle's owners.

353 top left The 16th-century Cabinet des Grelots is entirely covered with magnificent wood paneling and paintings depicting such subjects as hunting, music and games.

353 top right The great castle kitchen, with its hanging copper pans, is fascinating.

353 bottom right Joan of Arc is portrayed in the Galerie des Illustres.

354 and 355
The family of the
marquises de Vilbraye
lived in Cheverny
Castle for 300 years.
They retained intact
the majestic
proportions of the
rooms, the
magnificent
furnishings of the
king's chamber, as
well as the castle's
Gobelin tapestries
and paintings and
valuable prints.

A KING'S DREAM: CHAMBORD

Finally, we come to Chambord, a mirage from afar and a labyrinth to visit. Visitors should climb the Renaissance staircase, visit the rooms, go out onto the terraces, look down on the huge grounds and come as close as possible to the forest of pinnacles and turrets. This is how the megalomaniac dream of Francis I appears, in all its splendor. That ambitious king, with his ardent temperament and craving for novelty, glory and splendor, concluded his architectural dreams here. Numbers are not everything, but they give some idea of the scale of this magnificent site: 440 rooms, 80 staircases and 365 fireplaces surrounded by about 13,750 acres of perfectly rectangular grounds (about 3,750 of which are open to the public) crowded with deer and wild boar and surrounded by boundary walls about 20 miles long. Chambord is without doubt the most extravagant, exaggerated and majestic castle in the entire Loire Valley. Plundered during the Revolution, belonged then to Marshal Berthier and to the dukes of Bordeaux, then taken over by the government in 1930, Chambord Castle is the unrivaled star of the Loire Valley. Above all it is a hymn to grandeur; with its tufa and slate roof resembling a hanging garden and a thousand pillars, pinnacles, chimney pots and skylights, it would come as no surprise to see fairies or impudent gnomes gamboling there.

356 and 357 The impressive Chambord Castle is the largest in Sologne; it stands not far from Blois, and is surrounded by a huge, ancient park. Its construction was started by order of Francis I, and completed during the reign of Louis XIV, the Sun King. Not all the rooms in Chambord Castle are furnished, but some of them contain a series of late 16th-century Paris tapestries portraying scenes of the king's hunt, woven following cartoons by Laurent Guyot.

357 top This detail of one of the decorations that frame the tapestries of Chambord recalls motifs with a clearly neoclassical inspiration.

358-359 The twin circular staircase, about 9 yards wide, is the heart of the great castle; two people can go up or down it without meeting. The staircase, with its Renaissance design, terminates at the top with a coffered vault engraved with a salamander, the emblem of Francis I.

359 top left The rectangular chapel on the first floor, situated in a round tower, is the largest room in the castle. It was begun by Francis I and finished under Louis XIV by architect Harduin-Mansart.

359 top right The furnishings of Chambord Castle are luxurious, and great attention is paid to every detail, as demonstrated by this radiator covered with blue and white majolica in the best Flemish tradition.

360 and 361 The Queen's Room, the King's Room and the rooms of the Count of Chambord in Chambord Castle are furnished with valuable furniture, Amiens tapestries, four-poster beds and exquisite carpets.

The luxury exuded by these noble chambers is not reflected in all of the more than 400 rooms in the castle; Francis I's somewhat megalomanic dream of creating the most spectacular, majestic, regal castle in France was brought to an end by the revolution of 1789, during which Chambord was stripped of much of its finery. However, what remains clearly shows how magnificent it must have been at the height of its glory.

361

362 Among the most famous portraits at Chambord are those of the castle's founder, Francis I (top left), Henri IV (top right), Louis XIV (bottom left), and Stanislaw Leczinski, king of Poland and duke of Bar and Lorraine (bottom right).

362-363 The Salle de Compagnie at Chambord Castle contains a magnificent collection of portraits of outstanding personalities from the reigning French monarchy and illustrious foreign guests.

363 bottom
This young face with an enigmatic smile belongs to Mlle de Blois, one of the most courted and powerful French women of the time.

364 top Montigny-le-
Gannelon Castle,
with its alternating
brick and stone
decoration and tall
slate roofs, dates from
the late 14th century,
when the defensive
structure was
beginning to be
replaced by the castle
residence, still
grandiose but more
worldly than military.

364-365 High above
the Loir River (not to
be confused with the
Loire), Châteaudun
Castle, with its
feudal bulk and slate
roofs, overlooks the
small town below.
A stronghold
demolished by the
Norman Rollon in
911 already existed
on the site in the 5th
century.

CASTLES AND THE REMEMBRANCE OF THINGS PAST

To the north of the Loire River, in the romantic heart of France, the great castles become few and far between. Here, the landscape has the fragrance of harvest time, the charm of deserted horizons and, to the west, already heralds the Normandy countryside, with its boundless greenery and pastures. This area contrasts sharply with the grandiose Loire Valley and its magnificent castles, but here, unspoiled nature and wide-open spaces still lead to lesser known castles, that are no less rich in memories and links with the history of the Loire Valley. The castle of Châteaudun is impressive for the steep crag on which it perches, and the castle of Montigny-le-Gannelon for its magnificent furnishings. Another king's mistress, Mme de Maintenon, leads the tour through the splendors of the castle named after her, while Diane de Poitiers lies in Anet Castle, and the dream of grandeur cherished by the marquis de Laborde sleeps at La Ferté-Vidame. Memories of Proust fill the country footpaths and lanes of Illiers-Combray against the distant background of Chartres and its huge cathedral, reaching for the sky.

365 At the end of a narrow street in the village of Illiers-Combray stands the small 19th-century middle-class home of Proust's aunt and uncle, where the famous author spent his Easter holidays as a boy. Everything has remained as it was recounted in À la Recherche du Temps Perdu – the inner garden with its rosebushes and hydrangeas and the author's bedroom are still there.

366-367 Montigny-le-Gannelon Castle, like nearly all those in the Loire Valley, stands on the remains of an ancient stronghold, this one dating from the 12th century and overlooking the Loir River. The prettier style of the building erected in the 14th century by Jacques de Renty, and frequently altered over the centuries, can be seen from the large entrance park. In 1831 the castle was bought by Prince Montmorency-Laval, who restored the side overlooking the grounds. His son-in-law, the duke of Lévis-Mirepoix, altered the façade overlooking the Loir River in neo-Gothic style and erected a separate building in Baltard style that contains a collection of ancient agricultural machinery.

MORE HALLS, STAIRCASES AND FORTIFIED WALLS: MONTIGNY-LE-GANNELON AND CHÂTEAUDUN

High above the Loir (not to be mistaken with the Loire), the castle of Montigny-le-Gannelon, already a fortress in the time of Charlemagne, acquired its present name in the year 1000 and its Renaissance style in the 16th century, under Louis XII, when Jacques de Renty demolished the ancient fortress to build a new residence in the contemporary style. All that remains of that project is the Ladies' Tower and the Clock Tower, which were later connected at the base by a Gothic gallery. The property passed through the hands of various owners, statesmen and princes, such as Adrien, lord of Montmorency, duke of Laval and Louis XVIII's ambassador to Rome, Madrid, London and Vienna, who is often mentioned during the visit. This visit is particularly interesting because it is conducted by a member of the present-day family of the viscounts of Talhouët Boisorhand, who live in the castle and know the history and legends of the area. The building was altered on various occasions; the last and most visible alteration was ordered by Count Sigismond de Lévis, who completely rebuilt the east façade overlooking the Loir in 1886.

366 top and 367 right The rooms in the castle, decorated in red, blue and gold, are full of priceless antique furniture and portraits of illustrious members of the family. The castle now belongs to the descendants of the family of viscount of Talhouët, who personally guide visitors through the castle, recounting its history and mysterious legends.

368 left The Gothic-Renaissance staircase leads to the large rooms on the second floor, hung with magnificent tapestries.

368 top right The dungeon, dating from the 12th century, has retained the amazing inner framework of exposed beams.

369 Châteaudun Castle belonged to the d'Orléans family, which extended, decorated, fortified and defended it against enemy attack for four centuries (from the 14th to 18th centuries). It was above all Jean

d'Orléans (known as "the Bastard" because he was the illegitimate son of Louis I d'Orléans) who undertook the building of the castle as it survives now, incorporating the tall keep.

368 bottom right Three different periods – feudal, Gothic and Renaissance – have given the castle its grandeur. The 12th-century keep is built onto the Sainte-Chapelle, part of the Dunois wing, dating from the 15th century, which is illuminated by large Gothic windows.

The 15 wooden statues in the chapel portray members of the d'Orléans family, carved in the images of saints and beatified personalities, like the tiny Saint Agnes and the Saint Francis, who are none other than Agnès of Savoy and François de Longueville.

Around 6 miles from Montigny-le-Gannelon, the towering bulk of another castle is reflected in the river: this is Châteaudun. The unusual design of the castle, which overlooks the main road to Alençon, is very impressive. However, for visitors arriving from the Chartres direction, the gray walls lose their severe look and acquire the harmony of a Renaissance mansion, with the staircase carved like lace, the great fireplaces, the chapel decorated with magnificent wooden statues, and the tapestries hanging in the reception room.

It was Jean le Dunois who first decided to give his home two faces, representing a compromise between the feudal past and the desire for a more modern residence. The Norman architect Colin du Val, who hailed from Longueville, built the decidedly Renaissance north wing (called the Dunois wing) between the 12th-century tower and the buttress overlooking the Loir. There is a magnificent view from the towers, and as the visit proceeds from room to room the guide tells the stories of Thibault the Trickster, who built the feudal castle (of which nothing now remains), and Jean le Dunois, loyal general of Charles VII and comrade in arms of Joan of Arc at the siege of Orléans, who was the guiding force behind Châteaudun.

370 top In Aunt Léonie's famous room (left) at Illiers-Combray, Proust (portrait on right) was overwhelmed by the memories evoked by a little madeleine dipped into the lime tea served by his aunt.

THE VILLAGE OF THE SWEET MADELEINE

*I*n the huge plain of Beauce, a bell tower pierces the sky like a sharp pencil. "It was the first thing to appear when the train was pulling in to Combray," wrote Proust in *À la Recherche du Temps Perdu*. The pages of his novel seem to turn at every step one takes in the village of Illiers-Combray, which has added the name invented by the author to its own. Here, Proust arrived to spend the Easter holidays at the small house at the bottom of the garden at 4, Rue Docteur-Proust, where many remembrances still remain along with the memory of the sweet, unforgettable madeleine.

Nothing has changed, and on the first floor, Aunt Léonie's room still evokes the atmosphere of that famous page where the author, from the flavor of the morsel of madeleine dipped into the lime tea, recalls past memories. From far off can be seen Chartres Cathedral, which celebrated its 800th anniversary in 1994. At sunset, in the twilit nave, the light sets fire to the reds and blues of the famous 13th-century windows illustrating the lives of the saints, the ancient trades of France, and many Bible stories. The small dark Virgin is venerated at the end of the left-hand aisle. The great statues covering the façade return in the bas-reliefs surrounding the high altar inside, commemorating the art of Jehan de Beauce, who carved the exceptional row of people at prayer in 1514. The still medieval part of the town clusters around the two asymmetrical bell towers in a network of narrow alleys. In the motionless peace of the countryside sleeps Senoches, capital of Perche, the region of good cider. From the small town romantic walks branch off into the nearby forest, around the pond of Lille and La Ferté-Vidame. Nestled in Thymerais Forest, this grandiose patrician residence, now in ruins, still evokes the splendors of the court of the marquis de Laborde, who built his palace in the 18th century on the foundations of the previous castle, where Duke Saint-Simon (author of *Les Mémoires*) lived. The castle was partly destroyed and plundered during the Revolution, and so it has remained until the present day. Fields and meadows protect the abandoned building, which was too large and too magnificent for its bygone splendor to be adequately restored. Maintenon Castle, with its 12th-century keep, the grace of the Renaissance wing and the neoclassical proportions of the side built by Louis XIV, still maintains its royal air. Surrounded by huge grounds, part of which have been sold to the most exclusive golf club in France, the castle was given by Louis XVI to his mistress, Mme de Maintenon, who later became his secret wife. Its drawing rooms and great halls, curtains, velvets, damasks and antique furniture all remain just as they were at the time when the famous lady of the court withdrew with her king to the calm countryside of Eure.

ANET CASTLE: THE TOMB OF BEAUTIFUL DIANE

372 left At the end of the last century the castle was restructured and decorated, and restoration work was carried out on the garden chapel, with its lovely Renaissance dome illuminating an inlaid marble floor that seems to reflect the ornamental motifs of the dome.

From Maintenon it is only a short distance to Anet Castle, the last piece in the huge mosaic of residences associated with the history of the Loire. It was built in 1550 by order of King Henri II, who gave it to his mistress, Diane de Poitiers, as their love nest. The message of this residence is apparent right from the entrance portal, a triumphal arch in honor of "Diana the Huntress," with the naked nymph sculpted by Benvenuto Cellini in the lunette; it was a refuge of pleasure, not a theater of war like many other châteaux of the Loire. The most enlightened minds of the time gathered at Anet, and the king and his mistress went hunting or walked in nearby Dreux Forest. The castle, like many others, was damaged and plundered during the Revolution. It was sold, the furniture was scattered, and part of the castle was demolished by unscrupulous purchasers. In 1820 it was bought by the duchess of Orléans and restored for the first time. However, it was to take years, until nearly the end of the century, before M. Moreau and his descendants restored the home so that it was worthy of the history it recounts. Now preciously decorated, each room evokes the memory of the king's lovely mistress. Four tapestries woven especially for her in 1552 decorate the Salle des

Gardes; other Flemish tapestries drape the walls of the room containing a fireplace decorated with an alabaster medallion by Jean Goujon; the four-poster bed with its canopy bears her initials and sentimental souvenirs belonging to Diane are displayed in the Red Room. In the courtyard is the entrance to Saint Thomas' Chapel. Diane's tomb is in the garden, behind the chapel. After the king's death, she took lonely refuge in this castle, where she lived until her death in 1566. Her last residence closes the romantic and dissolute history of the Loire Valley castles.

372 top and 372-373 Anet Castle was King Henri II's gift to his lovely mistress, Diane de Poitiers. Here the king and Diane retreated for short periods, far from the splendors and court intrigue characteristic of the castles closest to the Loire. The residence, situated on the edge of Dreux Forest, is a gem of secluded Renaissance beauty.

372 bottom right Diane de Poitiers (portrayed here as Diana the Huntress) retired to Anet after the death of King Henri II, when Catherine de Médicis took revenge by confiscating Chenonceau Castle.

373 The spirit of the beautiful Diane can be felt in every corner of the castle, from the splendid main staircase (top left) to the bedroom, with its decorations, tapestries, paintings and four-poster bed (top right), to the Salle des Gardes (center right), decorated with huge Fontainebleau tapestries, to the exquisite wood-paneled Red Room (bottom right).

GENERAL INDEX

Note: c = *caption*

PHOTO CREDITS

384 As a palace within a park, Nymphenburg is quite different from other compact palaces like Versailles.
The entire façade is designed to provide access to the park: the galleries that connect the two side wings open onto the gardens, and even the old central portion on the ground floor has wide passageways through which coaches once passed.